A SAINT FOR YOUR NAME

A Saint
for
Your Name

REVISED AND UPDATED

SAINTS FOR BOYS

ALBERT J. NEVINS, M.M.
REVISED BY
ANN BALL

Our Sunday Visitor Publishing Division
Our Sunday Visitor, Inc.
Huntington, Indiana 46750

Our Sunday Visitor Publishing Division
Our Sunday Visitor, Inc.
200 Noll Plaza
Huntington, IN 46750

ISBN: 0-87973-601-1
LCCCN: 79-92504

Illustrations by James McIlrath
Cover by Rebecca Heaston
Edited by Lisa Grote
Printed in the United States of America

CONTENTS

ST. ANTHONY OF PADUA
ONE OF THE MOST POPULAR SAINTS

What's in a Name?

It is a venerable and beautiful Christian custom to give children the name of a saint at Baptism. This saint is chosen to be a patron, a protector, and a model for the new Christian. At Confirmation, the child may take the name of another saint, an additional patron and model. This practice is highly recommended by the Church. As children learn the stories of their saints, they are encouraged to emulate the attributes of the saints and to pray to and request the saints' loving help in their daily life.

Where Do Names Come From?

Names were in existence long before anybody ever wrote them down. Customs regarding the bestowing of names have changed throughout the centuries. In America today, we come into the world with a family name, or surname, attached. Our parents give us another name as our own personal, or given, name. Sometimes they give us more than one given name. Friends and family often call us by a nickname.

The first family names came about in a number of ways. A man was often named after the place in which he lived, the work he did, or even from the main physical features of a wealthy landowner's property. A habit followed far and wide was to add the word "son" to the name of the father. Often, physical features such as a person's coloring contributed to the family name. When people emigrated to other countries, often those in the new countries could not pronounce the original names in the various languages of the new immigrants. Thus, many names were changed to blend with those in the new country. This was especially true in America, a land of immigrants. Persecution, too, has left its mark on family names. It was often dangerous for a man to keep his original name and thus he changed it to match his new situation. In America, our family name comes from our father, although immigrants from Spanish-speaking countries have brought their custom of adding their mother's family name after their father's surname.

Names are not fixed, but are changeable. Spelling is a matter of personal choice and the pronunciation of names often changes greatly, even within a single country.

GIVEN NAMES HAVE HISTORY AND MEANING

Many given names have come down to us from Greek and Latin words. Each of these words has meanings, and these same meanings are found in other languages. The Bible, too, has provided a wealth of given names. Names have been taken from nature, from famous people, and new names are constantly being derived from old ones. The nicknames, or familiar names we are known by among our families and friends, have often evolved into common given names. The word nickname is actually a slurred form of "an ekename." "Eke" is an old English word for "additional." So an ekename, or a nickname, is an extra name. In the same way that nicknames have sometimes become common given names, last names have also often become commonly used as first names.

Although the majority of American names came to us through the European traditions with the waves of European immigrants who came to the United States, many beautiful and meaningful names have come from other languages and traditions. A good case in point: the names often chosen today by African-Americans. They look to their roots to select meaningful names from the many and varied African languages. Many of these names have the same meanings as the European-based ones, though sounds may be different.*

The exact way a name is written is only a matter of tradition. There are many languages and several alphabets, so the same name may look quite different from one language to another. Saints' names can be transliterated from one language to another to give a fairly close approximation of the pronunciation of a name in its original language.

*In this book, we have omitted the diacritical markings of some names from other languages.

Bestowing Saints' Names

The custom of giving children the names of Christian saints dates from the first millennium. In the Frankish kingdoms (France and Germany), the people gave their children the names of Apostles, biblical saints, or the names of early martyrs or confessors. By the thirteenth century, this custom had spread throughout the European continent.

Originally, the Gaelic population of Ireland did not follow this custom, and there are no Christian names found in the ancient Irish documents. In early centuries, Irish parents did not give the names of saints to their children because of their devout and humble attitude. They considered it irreverent to claim such hallowed names for their own. Only after the advent of the Normans did the continental practice come into usage about the thirteenth century. Some Gaelic clans did, however, call themselves "servants" (gil, mal) of Christ and the saints. This custom affected their surnames rather than their given names. Gilmartin, for example, designated the servant of St. Martin, as the name Malone designated the servant of St. John.

Through a special feeling of reverence, all Christian nations except the Spanish-speaking people originally avoided giving their children the given name of Our Lord, Jesus. It is, however, customary and common to bestow this name on Hispanic boys. This same feeling of reverence has kept the popes from using the name of Peter, and caused the Irish to set apart the original name of Mary — Muire — never giving it to their daughters in this form.

In Spanish-speaking countries, it is a general custom to give girls not only the name of Mary but also some of her liturgical titles and attributes as names. Thus, names such as Luz (Our Lady of Light), Dolores (Our Lady of Sorrows), Concepción (The Immaculate Conception), or Stella (Star of the Sea), are common names for Hispanic girls. The Chaldeans and Syrians gave girls names of Mary that refer to her attributes such as Afifa (her purity), Farida (her uniqueness), or Kamala (her perfection.)

Although many parents today, even Christian ones, choose their children's names without regard to hallowed tradition, the Church still strongly recommends bestowing a saint's name in Baptism. If the chosen first name has no Christian origin or significance, the saint's name may be given as a middle name.

Different and Unusual Names

Parents today often create, or "make up," a name, preferring something new or unusual to the common or ordinary ones. There is nothing intrinsically wrong with this practice, although with a little research and study, parents can create beautiful and unique names with Christian meanings. Names from all languages have meanings, and names with Christian meanings can be found in all languages. The names Chinue, Ibo for "God's own blessing," Olufemi, Yoruba for "God loves me," Jamala, Chaldean for "the beauty of Mary," are three of many names which have meaning as well as uniqueness. Spelling varies widely and is a matter of personal choice. Thus the name Toby, from the Hebrew meaning "The Lord is Good," could be spelled Tobi for a name both unusual and meaningful.

Saints' Names

Although there are only about a thousand saints that have been officially canonized by the Catholic Church, there are more than four thousand saints generally recognized by the Church. Many of these saints come from the lists of ancient martyrologies. Biblical names are sometimes given as saints' names to children. In the last few years, this trend has accounted for several of the most popular names chosen in America. Benjamin, Jesse, and Joshua were among the top names for boys in the 1990s and all are names of Biblical heroes. In such a small book, therefore, we could not hope to include more than a sampling of the most popular saints' names.

Pope John Paul II, has beatified many new saints, holding up for us more saintly examples to imitate. Most often, these saints were given the name of a previous saint at Baptism. However, parents can name their children after these new saints using their Christian name, or choosing to use the saint's given name in his or her native language, or a derivative of this name. Blessed Kateri Tekakwitha, our new American Indian saint, was given the name Kateri after the great Catherine of Siena. Today, Kateri herself is held up for honor, so a girl could take the name Kateri, the Indian spelling of Katherine, or choose her Indian name, Tekakwitha.

Today, saints are most often canonized with their complete name, so a surname might be used as a given name to reflect the new saint.

Name Days

Before the Reformation, and even today in some Catholic countries, the general custom was to celebrate not so much a child's birthday but rather the feast of the saint whose name was received in Baptism. Although this practice has never been strong in American usage, it is a good custom to introduce. On the feast day of the child's saint, the family could attend Mass together and afterwards gather with family and friends for a private celebration. Congratulations and small gifts are given to the one who bears the name of the saint of the day. The story of the saint may be read and decorations and foods could carry out the theme of the attributes of the saint. The celebration of Name Days is a good way to emphasize the fact that our Catholic religion belongs in the home, not simply in church on Sunday.

Some Notes on This Revision

In this revision of Father Nevins's popular work, we have attempted to include the names and stories of some of the newly canonized saints, as well as the names of some of the *beati* who have special significance for Americans. We can begin honoring our new saints in the very special way of giving their names to today's children, in hopes that their stories will become better known and loved throughout the world.

As in the previous edition, there are separate books for boys' names and girls' names. A list in the back of each book can help you locate some of the different forms and spellings of these names. Sometimes, the names refer to an original name of the opposite gender. When known, the language and meaning of the name are given. If a date is shown, it refers to the feast day of the saint.

SAINTS FOR BOYS
(ALPHABETICAL LISTING)

AARON

(Hebrew: Lofty Mountain)
June 21

The name Aaron first appears in the Bible in the Book of Exodus. Aaron was the brother of Moses and a member of the tribe of Levi. With Moses he shared in the leadership of the people and often spoke to the people in the name of Moses. Like Moses, he never entered the Promised Land but died on the slopes of Mt. Hor. He was the first High Priest of the Israelites and was succeeded by his son, Eleazar.

ABRAHAM

14

ABRAHAM

(Hebrew: Father of Many)
October 9
Another Form: Abram

About 2,000 years before Christ, there lived a chieftain near the city of Ur in the land of the Chaldeans (Mesopotamia), whose name was Abram, which means "God is exalted." Abram was different from the people among whom he lived because, while they worshipped many gods, he worshipped the one, true God. Because of this, he was pleasing to God. One day he heard God's voice within himself saying, "Go forth from the land of your relatives to a land I will show you. I will bless you and make of you a great nation." Abram obeyed God and with his family and his flocks made the long journey to the land of Canaan, which today we know as Israel. God was pleased that Abram obeyed him and he changed Abram's name to Abraham, which means "father of many."

God had promised Abraham that his descendants "would be as many as the stars in the sky." Abraham did not know how this was to happen since he and his wife, Sarah, had no children. Then, unexpectedly, God sent Abraham a son, whom he named Isaac. He loved the boy greatly, and it was through Isaac that God was to test Abraham once more.

Again Abraham heard the voice of God. It said: "Abraham, take your son Isaac, your only one, whom you love, and offer him up as a sacrifice on a hill I will show you." Abraham was sad but he prepared to obey God. He took Isaac to the hill, made ready a fire, tied the boy, and laid him on the logs. He was ready to light the fire when a voice spoke from heaven, telling him to wait. The voice said that Abraham had proven his love for God by his willingness to give up his son. Isaac did not have to die. Once again God blessed Abraham and promised that he would be the father of a great people. Abraham is the ancestor of the Jewish and Arab peoples. He died at a very old age and was buried with his wife in a cave.

Some other saints with this name:

ST. ABRAHAM KIDUNNIA (MESOPOTAMIA)
March 16

St. Abraham of Carrhae (Syria)
February 14

St. Abraham of Rostov (Russia)
October 29

St. Abraham of Smolensk (Russia)
August 21

ADAM

(Hebrew: First of Earth)
December 24
Another Form: Adan

The Bible names Adam as the first human being on earth. He was created by God in a very special way. God also created Eve to be his wife and companion. God tested Adam and Eve, and because they failed the test, they lost, not only for themselves but for all mankind, many gifts which God would have given them. Adam is known as one of the patrons of gardeners.

Another saint with this name:

Blessed Adam of Loccum (Germany)
December 22

ADRIAN

(Greek: Brave)
September 8
Other Forms: Adrien, Hadrian

Adrian was a Roman officer (c. 300) who was stationed in what is now Turkey. One day twenty-three Christians were arrested and were beaten and tortured by the soldiers. Adrian was so moved by their suffering and bravery that he stepped forward and said: "Count me with these men, for I am also a Christian." Adrian was immediately arrested.

Along with other Christians, he was sentenced to have his arms and legs broken and then cut off. He died during the torture. Later the broken bodies were ordered burned, but a heavy rainstorm came up and put out the fire. Christians gathered the remains of Adrian and his companions and buried them. Later the relics were taken to Rome. Adrian became a very popular martyr and was named the patron of soldiers.

ALAN

(Celtic: Harmony)
September 8
Other Forms: Alain, Allan, Allen

Blessed Alan de la Roche was born in the Brittany area of France and from his earliest years had a great love of and devotion to the Virgin Mary. He entered the Dominican Order and soon won a reputation as a brilliant student. After being ordained a priest, he was assigned to promote devotion both to the Virgin Mary and the Rosary. He preached in France, Belgium, Denmark, and Holland. While working in Holland, he was taken ill on the Feast of the Assumption (August 15) and died there on the Feast of the Nativity of the Blessed Virgin (September 8), 1475.

ALBAN

(Latin: White)
June 22
Other Forms: Alben, Albin, Alva

St. Alban was the first martyr of Britain. He gave shelter to a priest who then converted Alban to Christianity. Alban was arrested during the persecution of Diocletian (about 303) at Verulam (the city was later renamed after him), where a famous abbey was built in his honor. Alban reconverted one of his jailers, who also died with him.

ST. ALBERT THE GREAT

ALBERT

(Teutonic: Illustrious)
November 15
Other Forms: Adalbert, Alberto, Albrecht, Bert, Dethert

St. Albert the Great is one of the most famous teachers of Christianity. He was born into a wealthy and powerful family in Germany that had big plans for him. Over their strong objections, Albert decided to become a priest and entered the Dominican Order in Italy. His brilliance and scholarship caused his superiors to send him to the University of Paris to teach and to get his master's degree. Students flocked to his classes, and one of them, Thomas of Aquino, also became a great philosopher and a saint. Albert returned to Cologne, where he continued to teach and write. His reputation for learning became so great that he was called Albert the Great even in his own lifetime. Against his objections he was made a bishop. He was in his eighties when he died on November 15, 1280. He was named a saint, a Doctor (Teacher) of the Church, and patron of scientists and philosophers.

Some other saints with this name:

ST. ALBERT OF CASHEL (IRELAND)
January 19

ST. ALBERT OF LOUVAIN (BELGIUM)
November 21

ALCUIN

(Teutonic: Noble Friend)
May 19

Blessed Alcuin was born in York, England, and became the head of a school there, winning a reputation as a scholar and teacher. He made several visits to Rome, and on one of them the Emperor Charlemagne invited him to become an adviser at the royal court. Later, Charlemagne appointed him head of a Benedictine abbey in France, where he continued his teaching and attracted many students from France and England. He died in 804.

ALEXANDER

(Greek: Helper of Men)
December 1
Other Forms: Alistair, Alec, Alex, Alejandro, Sacha, Sandor

Alexander Bryant was a popular and handsome student at Oxford University during the persecution of the Catholic Church by Queen

Elizabeth. Like most of the students, he had abandoned his Catholic religion in favor of the Anglican Church. However, while at Oxford and through the efforts of some secret Catholics, he was converted back to the Catholic faith and decided to become a priest. Since this was impossible in England, he went to the English seminary in Douay, France, where he was ordained in 1579. He smuggled himself back into England and began his ministry to hidden Catholics. After two years of work he was trapped by Queen Elizabeth's police in a house in London. He was imprisoned in the Tower of London, where he was tortured to make him reveal what he knew about other priests in England. Despite having needles thrust under his fingernails and being racked to the limit on two successive days, he revealed nothing. After a public trial, he was taken to Tyburn Hill, where he was hanged, drawn, and quartered. The date of his death is December 1, 1582. He was canonized in 1970 as one of the forty new English and Welsh saints.

Other saints with this name:

St. Alexander (Constantinople)
August 28

St. Alexander (Egypt)
February 26

St. Alexander (Jerusalem)
March 18

Alexis

(Greek: Helper)
July 17
Other Forms: Alex, Alexei

St. Alexis was the son of a Roman senator. Pledging himself to God, he fled his home rather than be forced into a marriage. He made his way to Asia Minor, where he lived as a hermit and busied himself with good works. Because of his holiness, people were attracted to him. This caused him to flee again. He eventually returned to Rome and found shelter in a shed on his father's estate without anyone knowing who he was. He spent his time in prayer and supported himself by begging. After his death, papers found on his body revealed his identity. Both the pope and the emperor attended his funeral in 404. Many miracles were credited to his intercession.

ALOYSIUS

(Latin: The Very Wise)
June 21
Other Forms: Aloys, Aluigi

Aloysius Gonzaga was born into a noble Italian family in 1568. His father wanted him to have a military career and, when the boy was only four years old, dressed him as a soldier and made him mix with troops he was organizing for the king of Spain. Aloysius learned some dirty words from the soldiers and used them, a fact that embarrassed him for the rest of his life. When he was seven he decided to devote himself to God and at age eleven made a vow of perpetual chastity. His father forced him to serve at various royal courts, refusing to let him follow a religious vocation. When he was seventeen, he entered the Society of Jesus, where he quickly won a reputation for innocence and sanctity. He died when he was only twenty-three years old. He is a patron of youth.

ALPHONSE

(Teutonic: Eager for Battle)
August 1
Other Forms: Alfonso, Alonzo, Lon, Lonnie

St. Alphonsus Liguori was born into a pious family in Naples, Italy, in 1696. Of nine children in the family, three boys became priests and two girls became nuns. Alphonsus did not plan to become a priest. A brilliant student, he graduated with a law degree when only sixteen years old. His legal skills were much in demand, and his career prospered. When he was twenty-seven years old, he lost a case and felt so bad about it that he began to look into the values of his life. He decided that he should use his talents solely for God and thus became a priest.

He first worked among the poor in the countryside around Naples but realized that there was so much to be done that he needed help. He founded the Redemptorist Congregation, which spread rapidly and not too long after his death even reached America. St. Alphonsus became a bishop but later resigned to live in his congregation. He was more than ninety years old when he died. One spiritual gift he received was bilocation, the ability to be in two places at once. On September 21, 1774, when he was in his bishopric of Sant' Agata de Goti, he also appeared in Rome to comfort the dying Pope Clement XIV. He is the patron of confessors.

AMBROSE

(Greek: Immortal)
December 7

St. Ambrose is thought to have been born in Trier, Germany, where his father was prefect of Gaul. He himself entered the service of the Roman Empire and eventually became governor of a province centered in Milan, Italy. While he was ruling there, the bishop died. The people could not agree who should be the new bishop until someone proposed Ambrose's name and he was immediately elected. Ambrose was only studying to be a Christian, but within a few days he was baptized and ordained a priest and made a bishop. The young nobleman became the advisor to three Roman emperors. He was known for his brilliance in preaching. A young African, Augustine of Hippo, heard him preach one day, was converted to the Catholic Church, and became the famous St. Augustine. St. Ambrose wrote many theological works, and some of his hymns are still sung in church today. He died in 397. He is the protector of bees and domestic animals.

Other saints with this name:

ST. AMBROSE BARLOW (ENGLAND)
October 25

ST. AMBROSE KIBUUKE (UGANDA)
June 3

AMOS

(Hebrew: Brave)
March 31

Amos was one of the twelve minor prophets of the Old Testament. He lived in Judah, near Bethlehem, and describes himself, in the book of the Bible that bears his name, as a herdsman and as one who cares for trees. He was called by God to preach repentance to the Northern Kingdom. He went to Bethel and Samaria and preached against the moral conditions he found. His prophetic mission lasted about a year.

ANDREW

(Greek: Manly)
November 30
Other forms: Andre, Andreas, Andres, Drew

Andrew the Apostle belonged to a family of fishermen of Capernaum, a town on the Sea of Galilee. Andrew was also a disciple of John the Baptist and was with John at the Jordan River when Jesus Christ came to be baptized. Hearing John praise Jesus, Andrew sought Him out and stayed with Him for a time. He also introduced Jesus to his brother, Simon Peter. When it came time for Jesus to form His band of Apostles, He went to Capernaum and selected Andrew and Simon Peter as His first Apostles. Andrew remained close to Jesus and an important member of the apostolic band. At the time when five thousand people were with Jesus with nothing to eat, it was Andrew who told Jesus about the boy with a few loaves of bread and some fish, which Jesus multiplied to feed the crowd. Tradition says that Andrew preached the Gospel around the Black Sea, where he was martyred on a cross in the shape of an X. He is the patron of fishermen, fish dealers, and women who wish to become mothers.

ST. ANDREW KIM
September 20

Father Kim Tae-gon Andrew was the first native Korean priest. After three months of imprisonment, he was beheaded on September

16, 1846. Just twenty-six years old at the time of his death, he made a farewell sermon saying "My eternal life is beginning now," and he calmly and courageously received the glorious crown of martyrdom.

Other saints by this name:

St. Andrew Avellino (Italy)
November 10

St. Andrew Bobola (Poland)
May 16

St. Andrew Kaqqwa (Uganda)
June 3

St. Andrew

ANGELO

(Greek: Messenger; Italian: Angel)
May 5
Another Form: Angel

St. Angelo was born in Jerusalem of Jewish parents who had been converted to Christianity. He and his brother became Carmelite monks. For five years he lived as a hermit on Mt. Carmel, and then he went to Sicily to preach the Gospel. He converted many Jews. In the course of his preaching, he denounced a wealthy and powerful man who led a very evil life. One day in 1220, when St. Angelo was preaching to a crowd of Sicilians, this man and some followers broke through the crowd and stabbed St. Angelo to death. As he lay dying, he prayed for the people of Sicily and forgave his murderer.

ANSELM

(Teutonic: Divine Helmet)
April 21
Other Forms: Ansel, Anselmo, Hansel

St. Anselm was born in northern Italy about 1033. His family was prominent and had royal connections. As a boy Anselm wanted to be a priest, but his father would not allow this. Instead, his father introduced him to court life and the young man enjoyed the pleasures of easy living. After the death of his mother, Anselm and his father quarreled. Anselm left home and made his way to France. For several years he drifted without purpose before the idea of the priesthood returned to him. He entered the Abbey of Bec in Normandy and became a monk. He quickly won a reputation throughout Europe for his learning and holiness. He became the abbot of his monastery and had to go frequently to England on business. During one trip, King William Rufus of England asked him to become bishop of Canterbury, and he remained in this post until his death in 1109. Because of his writings on philosophy and theology and the many prayers he composed, St. Anselm is ranked as a Doctor (Teacher) of the Church.

ANTHONY

(Greek: Priceless)
Other Forms: Antoine, Anton, Antonio, Antony, Tony

ST. ANTHONY OF EGYPT
January 17

Anthony was born in Upper Egypt about 250. When he was twenty, his parents died, leaving him with much property and wealth. After providing for his sister, he gave away all his money and went into the desert as a hermit. Despite his wish to be alone with God, people came to him with their troubles, and he is said to have worked miraculous cures for them. Disciples also sought him out, and he founded two monasteries. He died at the age of 105 in the cave that was his last home. St. Anthony is called the "father of monasticism."

ST. ANTHONY OF PADUA
June 13

Born in Lisbon, Portugal, in 1195, St. Anthony was twenty-five years old when the bodies of the first Franciscan martyrs were brought back from Africa for burial. He was so impressed by the sacrifice of these men that he joined the Franciscans and set out for Africa in the hope of finding martyrdom. He became sick, however, and had to return home. On the way back to Europe a storm forced his boat to Sicily. Here he joined some other Franciscans going to their headquarters in Italy. No one there expected him and he was left pretty much on his own. He lived in a cave near a monastery in Forli, coming out only for prayers and to sweep the monastery. One day a monk who was to preach to the community failed to appear and some of the members, probably as a joke, asked the young sweeper to take his place. Without any preparation Anthony gave a sermon that revealed both his theological knowledge and preaching skill. From that day on, he spent his life preaching throughout Italy, France, and Belgium. One day when the people would not listen to him, in imitation of St. Francis, he preached to fish which came to the surface of the water to hear his sermon. When the people saw this miracle, they were sorry they had not listened to Anthony. He

St. Anthony of Egypt

was very famous when he died at the age of thirty-six in Padua, Italy. St. Anthony is a Doctor (Teacher) of the Church and is often prayed to for the protection of horses and to find lost objects.

Born in Normandy, France, in 1601, St. Anthony Daniel was studying law when he decided to become a Jesuit. After training, he was sent to Canada to work among the Huron Indians. On July 4, 1648, he was just finishing Mass at St. Joseph's Mission when the village was raided by Iroquois Indians. Dipping his handkerchief in water, he baptized as many catechumens as he could, urging the Christians to flee to safety. He then went out to meet the Iroquois, hoping to gain more time for his Christians to escape. The invaders showered him with arrows. The Iroquois dragged his body into the church, which was then set on fire.

Another saint with this name:

ST. ANTHONY CLARET (SPAIN)
October 24

ARNOLD

(Teutonic: Strength of an Eagle)
July 8
Other Forms: Arnaldo, Arnoldo

St. Arnold was a Greek by birth who became a member of the court of the Emperor Charlemagne. He led a very holy life and was called a "model of Christian virtue." He was also known for his devotion to the poor. He died shortly after the year 800, and a village in France still bears his name.

AUGUSTINE

(Diminutive of Augustus, Latin: Majestic)
August 28
Other Forms: Agostino, August, Augustin, Austin

St. Augustine was born in North Africa in 354. His father, Patrick, was a pagan who was baptized on his deathbed. His mother was St.

Monica. Monica instructed her son in Christianity but he had no interest in religion. From the time he was sixteen he led a sensual life. He took up with a woman by whom he had a son named Adeodatus. A brilliant teacher, Augustine first taught in Carthage and then went to Italy to teach in Milan. He heard a sermon by St. Ambrose and was so moved that he went to him, began restudying Christianity, and was finally baptized by Ambrose, along with Adeodatus. During all these years, Monica had been praying for his conversion. After the death of St. Monica, who had accompanied him to Italy, Augustine returned to Africa. He sold his estates, gave the money to the poor, and began studies for the priesthood. After he was ordained he was assigned to a church in Hippo, where he gained fame as a preacher. In 396 he became Bishop of Hippo and spent the next thirty-five years preaching, writing, and governing his diocese. He died on August 28, 430, while the Vandals were storming Hippo during the fall of the Roman Empire. He was one of the Church's greatest theologians, and almost a hundred of his books and more than two hundred letters have survived. Also, more than four hundred of his sermons have been preserved. He is a Doctor (Teacher) of the Church.

Other saints with this name.

St. Augustine of Canterbury (England)
May 28

Blessed Augustine Chapdelaine (Vietnam)
February 28

Barnabas

(Hebrew: Son of Consolation)
June 11
Other Forms: Barnaby, Barney

Barnabas was a Jew of the tribe of Levi, a native of the island of Cyprus. He was in Jerusalem about the time of the first Pentecost, was converted, sold a field, and placed the money at the feet of the Apostles to be used for the Christian community. He was a friend of St. Paul, making missionary journeys with him. He also traveled to preach the Gospel with John Mark. He took part in the Council of Jerusalem. Tradition says that he was stoned to death in Salamis by Jews from Syria.

BARTHOLOMEW

(Hebrew: Son of Talmai)
August 24
Other Forms: Bart, Bartel, Bartolomeo, Barry

Bartholomew is listed in the Gospels and Acts as one of the Twelve Apostles. His name is always linked to that of Philip, who is thought to have been a close friend. He is also believed to be the one who is sometimes called Nathaniel. He was brought to Jesus by Philip and from that time on followed the Lord. He was present when Jesus appeared on the shore of the Sea of Galilee to eat bread and fish with His disciples. Tradition says that he preached the Gospel "in nearer India." He is the patron of butchers, tanners, and bookbinders.

BASIL

(Greek: Royal)
January 2
Other Forms: Vasily, Vassily

St. Basil the Great is honored as a Doctor (Teacher) of the Church in both the Greek and Latin Churches. He was one of the great figures of early Christianity. He is considered, along with St. Gregory Nazianzen, as the greatest of the Greek Fathers. He was born in 330 of Christian parents in Asia Minor. Early in life he desired to lead an ascetic life given to study and writing. He resisted Arianism and wrote much against the heresy. Because of his wisdom and holiness, he was made Bishop of Caesarea in 370. He wrote a monastic rule which is still followed today in the Eastern Churches, being to the East what St. Benedict's rule was to the West. Worn out by work and penances, he died at forty-nine years of age, January 1, 379.

BEDE

(Celtic: Life)
May 27

One writer has called St. Bede "the brightest ornament of the English nation." He was born in Northumbria in 673. He entered the monastery at Jarrow and was educated there, becoming a priest. He was a master of Latin and Greek, and his writings show his interest in many different subjects. He wrote a history of the English Church, which is a valuable record, and because of this he is called "Father of English Historians." He was the foremost scholar and teacher of his time. He died on the eve of the Ascension in 735, and his last words were "Glory be to the Father and the Son and the Holy Spirit." He was buried with great honor in Durham Cathedral. Called "Venerable" for centuries, he has been named Doctor (Teacher) of the Church.

BENEDICT

(Latin: Blessing)
July 11
Other Forms: Benedetto, Benoit, Bennett

St. Benedict, the father of modern monasticism and founder of the Benedictine Order, is one of the great figures of the Church. He was born in Umbria in what is now Italy. As a youth he went to Rome to study, but seeing the sinful habits of his fellow students and fearing he himself might be led into sin, he fled into the mountains around Subiaco, where he lived in a cave. Although he was removed from the world, his reputation for holiness and his wisdom caused others to go to him for spiritual direction.

Gradually a small band of monks formed about him. One day, Benedict and his followers left Subiaco and went to Monte Cassino, where there was a sacred grove of trees with altars to Apollo, Jupiter, and Venus. Benedict smashed the altars and set the grove on fire to destroy the last remains of paganism. He and his companions built a monastery there, which has grown great through the centuries. Benedict drew up a rule for his community which had for its motto "to work is to pray." His monasteries spread throughout Europe, and many cities grew up around them. He died in 543. Pope Pius XII called St. Benedict "The Father of Europe." He is prayed to against kidney disease and temptations of the devil.

Other saints with this name:

St. Benedict the Black (Italy)
April 4

ST. BENEDICT

BENJAMIN

(Hebrew: Son of the Right Hand)
March 31
Another Form: Ben, Benson

Benjamin is an ancient name appearing first in the story of Joseph in Egypt in the Book of Genesis. Benjamin was Joseph's youngest brother, the son of the patriarch Jacob. The saint with this name lived in Persia and was a deacon who preached Christianity. The pagan king ordered Benjamin to stop his preaching against the magi and fire worshippers of Persia. Benjamin refused to do so, and the king had him arrested. Despite many tortures to get him to deny his faith, Benjamin remained firm in his trust in God. Furious at his failure, the king ordered Benjamin executed (about 420).

BERNARD

(German: Bold as a Bear)
May 28
Other Forms: Barnard, Bernadino, Bernardo, Bernhard, Nardo

St. Bernard of Menthon was the founder of two famous Swiss hospices that saved the lives of many travelers. French and German pilgrims on the way to Rome crossed into Italy over two Alpine passes that were subject to unseasonal snowstorms. Many pilgrims caught in such storms became lost in snowdrifts and froze to death. To help these pilgrims, St. Bernard founded a hospice on each of the two main passes which became known as Great and Little St. Bernard. Monks were trained to seek pilgrims lost in the storm and bring them to safety and shelter in the hospices. A special breed of dog was developed to aid in this work, and this dog is today our huge St. Bernard dog. St. Bernard died in 1081. Pope Pius XI named him patron of mountain climbers.

Another saint with this name:

ST. BERNARD OF CLAIRVAUX (FRANCE)
August 20

BLASE

(Latin: Babbler)
February 3
Another Form: Blaise

St. Blase was the Bishop of Sebaste in Armenia. He once saved a boy from choking to death and for this reason is invoked against diseases of the throat. He was arrested under Licinius for being the chief of the Christians. He was tortured and beheaded in Sebaste in 316. His feast became popular in Asia Minor and was brought to Europe by the Crusaders. On his feast day throats are blessed, seeking the intercession of St. Blase.

BONAVENTURE

(Latin: Good Attempt)
July 15

St. Bonaventure is popularly known as the Seraphic Doctor. He was born in Italy in 1231. At the age of twenty, he entered the Franciscan Order, and after he was ordained a priest, he became a teacher. Along with St. Thomas Aquinas, he was a professor at the University of Paris. He was later elected Superior General of the Franciscans, and when his term was up, Pope Gregory X named him bishop of Albano and a cardinal. He died in 1274 during the Council of Lyons. He wrote many books of scholarship and also a popular life of St. Francis. Because of his learning and writings, he was named a Doctor (Teacher) of the Church.

BONIFACE

(Latin: Doer of Good Things)
June 5

Although known as the Apostle of Germany, Boniface was born in England about 680. He entered the abbey at Exeter as a boy and for some years taught other monks. His dream was to convert Germany. He finally received permission to go to Rome and propose a mission to

Germany. Pope Gregory II received him kindly, commissioned him as a missioner to Germany, made him a bishop, and changed his name from Winifrid to Boniface. Arriving in Germany, Boniface went directly to the center of pagan worship. The Germans believed that their god, Thor, resided in a sacred oak tree. Boniface chopped the tree down and began to preach Christianity. Boniface erected bishoprics, founded monasteries and churches, and brought many missioners from England to teach the Germans. In 755, when he was seventy-five, while on a mission journey, his band was attacked by pagans, and he was killed by a blow to the head. He was buried at the monastery in Fulda which he founded and where his relics can be seen today.

ST. BONIFACE

BRENDAN

(Celtic: Sword)
May 16
Other Forms: Brenden, Brandon, Brennan

St. Brendan was born in County Kerry, Ireland. He built several churches in that area. He founded a monastery at Clonfert and made many journeys, particularly to Britain. A book appearing after his death, called *Navigatio*, was supposedly written by him and tells of some of these journeys, which Brendan made in a leather boat. Students of the book claim that it shows Brendan reached Iceland and America. It is said that Columbus was familiar with the book and that it inspired him to seek the land discovered by St. Brendan. The book also tells about the monks who followed St. Brendan and lived his rule of life. He died at Clonfert about 580.

BRIAN

(Celtic: Strong)
December 10
Other Forms: Bryan, Bryant, Bryon, Byron

Blessed Brian Lacey was one of the Catholic martyrs put to death by the English in London in 1591. He is described as "a gentleman from Yorkshire." He was betrayed to the authorities by his own brother for aiding an underground priest, Father Montford Scott. He was tortured, and when he refused to deny the Catholic religion, he was sentenced to death. He was executed at Tyburn Prison on December 10, 1591.

BRICE

(Anglo Saxon: Breach)
November 13
Other Forms: Bruce, Bryce

St. Brice was an orphan who was rescued as a child by St. Martin of Tours. Growing up, he was proud, ungrateful, and a great trial to St.

Martin, who was often urged to send him packing. St. Martin refused, saying that God's grace would change Brice. St. Martin was right. Brice changed, became a bishop, had many trials but remained faithful to God. He is the patron for those who suffer stomach disorders. He died in 444.

BRUNO

(Teutonic: Brown)
October 6

St. Bruno was born into a noble family in Cologne, Germany, about 1035. He was a brilliant student and soon became one of the foremost theologians of his day. One of his students was the future Pope Urban II. Bruno was in line to become a bishop, but worldly honors meant nothing to him. With some friends he retired to a remote area and founded the Carthusian Order. Pope Urban II called him to Rome as an advisor. Bruno obeyed and went but was not happy at the papal court. The pope, in an attempt to keep him, offered to make him an archbishop. Bruno declined and the pope allowed him to go to Calabria and begin a new Carthusian monastery. He died a holy death in 1101.

Another saint with this name:

BRUNO SERINKUMA (UGANDA)
June 3

CAMILLUS

(Latin: Temple Servant)
July 14
Another Form: Camille, Camillo

St. Camillus de Lellis was born in southern Italy in 1550. After some years of worldly life, he decided to devote himself to the sick. He became a priest, gathered some followers, and founded a religious order whose members were pledged to care for the sick. He died in 1614.

CASIMIR

(Slavic: Peaceful)
March 4
Other Forms: Cass, Casper

Casimir was the third child born to King Casimir III of Poland. His birthday is October 5, 1458. From an early age he was given to prayer and desired nothing more than to become a saint. The young prince slept on the floor rather than in his comfortable bed, wore a hair shirt, and practiced many penances. Prince Casimir was offered the crown of Hungary but turned it down because he felt it belonged to another. He governed Poland from 1481 to 1483 while his father was away in Lithuania. During this time an attempt was made to have him marry the daughter of the emperor of Germany. He refused because he had privately made a vow of chastity. He died at age twenty-four, on March 5, 1484. He is known for his devotion to the Eucharist and the Virgin Mary. He was buried with his favorite hymn to Mary in his hands.

CEFERINO

(Latin: Small Rock)
May 4

Blessed Ceferino Gimenez Malla was a gypsy layman martyred in Spain in 1936, called "El Pele" (the fighter) by his people. Ceferino was an illiterate but well-respected horse dealer. He was sought as counsel for the poor and the politically powerful, and was revered as a pious Catholic. In July, 1936, he protested the arrest of a priest by the Spanish revolutionary militia and was taken prisoner. When he refused to quit reciting the Rosary, he was shot to death on August 2.

CHAD

(Celtic: Martial)
March 2

Chad was a monk in a monastery in Ireland before being appointed abbot of a monastery at Lastingham, England. Shortly afterwards, the bishop of the area died, and Chad was selected to succeed him. Later he was transferred and became bishop of Litchfield. He had a great love for the poor and spent much time among them. When the archbishop told him that he should travel about his diocese on horseback, Chad replied that he wished to imitate the Apostles by going about on foot. He died in 872, a victim of the plague.

CHARLES

(Teutonic: Strong)
November 4
Other Forms: Carl, Carlo, Carlos, Carroll, Caryl, Karl, Karol

When he was born October 2, 1538, into a wealthy Italian family, Charles Borromeo was an unlikely candidate for sainthood. He attended the best schools, and his personable manner made him popular among the rich and powerful. His uncle became Pope Pius IV and almost immediately made Charles, then only twenty-two, a cardinal and archbishop of Milan. He took up residence at the Roman court, where he had much influence in the Council of Trent. His brother's death in 1562 deeply affected him. Although he led a good life, he now began to lead a holy one. He was ordained a priest, returned to his archdiocese, and set about reforming it. He used his own money to found seminaries, schools, and hospitals, and during a great plague he went about the streets aiding the dying. He fasted on bread and water, slept on the ground, and gave his fortune to the poor. He died when only forty-six.

Other saints with this name:

St. Charles Lwanga (Uganda)
June 3

St. Charles Gamier (Canada)
September 26

CHRISTIAN

(Latin: Belonging to Christ)
June 12

St. Christian was an Irish bishop, brother of St. Malachy of Armagh. He was made bishop of Clogher in 1126. He led a holy life and was devoted to the care of the people of his diocese. He died in 1138.

ST. CHRISTOPHER

CHRISTOPHER

(Greek: Christ-bearer)
July 25
Other Forms: Chris, Christophe, Cristobal, Cristobalito, Cristoforo

St. Christopher was one of the most popular saints in the Middle Ages, and devotion to him continues to this day. He is said to have lived about 250. In the Greek Church he is honored as being martyred in Lycia during the persecution of Christianity by Decius. There are many legends of him in the Latin Church, the chief one that he became a ferryman who helped people across a turbulent river. He did this as a charitable work for Christ. One night he was hailed by a child, and as he carried the little boy across the stream, he learned he was carrying the Christ Child. St. Christopher is the patron of travelers, fruit dealers, and archers. His aid is invoked against sudden death and storms.

BLESSED CRISTOBALITO

Blesseds Cristobalito, Antonio, and Juan are known as the child martyrs of Tlaxcala, Mexico. They were three young Christian converts at the time the Catholic faith was introduced into Mexico. They were killed in hatred of the faith sometime between 1527 and 1529, and are believed to be the first laymen to be martyred in the New World.

Other saints with this name:

ST. CHRISTOPHER OF CORDOVA (SPAIN)
August 20

ST. CHRISTOPHER BUXTON (ENGLAND)
October 1

CLAIR

(Latin: Clear)
November 4
Other Forms: Clare, Clarus

St. Clair was an Englishman of noble birth who was born at Rochester. He became a priest and went to France to live in a hermitage. A noblewoman made advances to him, and when he rejected her, she had her thugs behead him in revenge. The dates of his life are uncertain, but he lived about the eighth century.

CLARENCE

(Latin: Illustrious)
April 26

Very little is known of St. Clarence other than that he succeeded St. Aetherius as bishop of Vienne (France). He died about 620.

CLAUDE

(Latin: Lame)
March 10
Other Forms: Claudius, Cloud

St. Claude was a member of a Roman legion stationed in Sebaste in Asia Minor. During the persecution of the Emperor Licinius, forty members of this legion were put to death when they refused to sacrifice to the Roman gods because they were Christians. Claude and his companions were stripped and left naked overnight on a frozen lake. The next morning their legs were broken, and they were cremated.

Another saint with this name:

ST. CLAUDE OF VIENNA (AUSTRIA)
June 1

CLEMENT

(Latin: Merciful)
November 23

Clement was the third pope after St. Peter to rule the Church. Some think he was Jewish; others believe he was a Roman. The basilica named after him in Rome is said to have been built over his house, where St. Peter often stayed. He wrote a famous letter to the Corinthians that is one of the most important documents of early Church history because it showed the importance of the papacy even at the end of the first century. The Church honors him as a martyr. He is the patron of boatmen and is prayed to for sick children.

Another saint with this name:

ST. CLEMENT MARY HOFBAUER (AUSTRIA)
March 15

COLMAN

(Irish: Short for Columba or Columban)
July 8

There are more than a hundred Irish saints named Colman. One of the best known was a missioner who left Ireland to preach the Gospel to the German tribes of Thuringia. Along with his companion missioners, Kilian and Tonan, he was martyred there for his labors about 690.

Other saints with this name:

ST. COLMAN OF CLOINE
November 26

ST. COLMAN OF LINDISFARNE
February 18

COLUMBA

(Gaelic from the Latin: Dove)
Other Forms: Cole, Coleman, Colin, Collin, Colton, Colum, Columban, Columbanus, Columcille, Cullen

ST. COLUMBA
June 9

While there are a number of saints by this name, the one best known is St. Columba of Iona. Like Columban, he was Irish and a great figure of Western monasticism. He founded a hundred monasteries and spent the last thirty-four years of his life as a missioner in Scotland, dying there in 597 at the monastery of Iona that he founded.

ST. COLUMBAN
November 23

St. Columban was born in Ireland about 540. He took his early training in the monastery at Bangor under St. Congall. Because of his learning, he was invited by the king of Burgundy (France) to preach the Gospel there. He took twelve monks and landed in France in 590. He founded many monasteries, but the one at Luxeuil had the greatest influence, educating many bishops and missioners. He had great influence throughout Europe, and among the many reforms he introduced was the Irish practice of private confession. He founded his last monastery at Bobbio in Italy and died there the following year.

CONSTANTINE

(Latin: Firm)
March 11
Other Forms: Connie, Constantius

St. Constantine was a Cornish prince who gave up his crown to become a monk. He founded a monastery at Govan on the Clyde River and worked to convert the area. He gave his life for the faith in 576.

CORMAC

(Celtic: Charioteer)
September 14

St. Cormac is listed as the first bishop of Cashel (Ireland). He put together the famous Cashel Psalter, a book of psalms. He was also king of Munster and died in battle in 908.

CORNELIUS

(Latin: Horn)
Other Forms: Connor, Conor, Corneal, Neal, Neil

ST. CORNELIUS THE CENTURION
February 2

Cornelius was a Roman officer, a centurion, who was in charge of the Italian Cohort stationed at Caesarea in the Holy Land. Some think he may have been the same centurion whose servant was healed by Jesus, who had helped build the synagogue at Capernaum. At any event, the Acts of the Apostles tells us that he had a vision that instructed him to send to Joppa for Simon Peter. St. Peter came and taught Cornelius about Jesus. He baptized Cornelius, his family, and some of his friends. The incident is important in Church history because it was the first Baptism of Gentiles by Peter. You can read the story in chapter ten of the Acts of the Apostles.

ST. CORNELIUS, POPE
September 18

Cornelius was ordained bishop of Rome and made pope in 251. He had to oppose enemies both within and outside the Church. He was sent into exile by the Emperor Gallus and died in 253 after a short reign as pope. His body was taken back to Rome and buried in the catacomb of St. Callistus. Because of his sufferings, the Church considers him a martyr. His name is listed in the first Eucharistic Prayer (the Roman Canon).

CYRIL

(Greek: Lordly)
Other Forms: Cyr, Cyriac, Kyle, Kyril

ST. CYRIL OF JERUSALEM
March 18

St. Cyril of Jerusalem is one of the Fathers and Doctors (Teachers) of the Church. He was born in Palestine and became bishop of Jerusalem about 350. He had a difficult life, being driven from his bishopric by Arian heretics and emperors who favored the heresy in an attempt to divide the Church. He wrote a catechism, which has come down to us, that he used to prepare new Christians for Baptism. He died about 387.

ST. CYRIL OF ALEXANDRIA
June 27

St. Cyril of Alexandria was also a Doctor (Teacher) of the Church. He was born in Egypt in 370. He entered a monastery, became a priest, and finally became bishop of Alexandria. He too had to fight against heretics. He was a leader at the Council of Ephesus and wrote many books to defend the Church. He was one of the earliest to defend the truth that Mary is the Mother of God. He died in 444.

BLESSED CYRIAC ELIAS CHAVARA
January 3

Blessed Cyriac was a Carmelite visionary and founder and a devoted son of the Blessed Virgin Mother of God. He is a model of the fervent charity of Christ. A member of the Syro-Malabar Catholic rite, he instituted a ministry fitted to his era and his region of the world. His congregation became the largest in India. He died January 3, 1871, after a long illness and was beatified in India in 1986.

DAMIAN

(Greek: Tamer)
September 26
Other Forms: Damiano, Damien, Damon

St. Damian with his brother, St. Cosmas, went from Arabia to Syria to practice medicine. They followed the Gospel command to give freely of their gifts. As a result of their medical mission, they won many converts. Because of this, they came to the attention of Lysias, who had been ordered by the emperor to hunt out Christians. Lysias had them arrested and ordered them to sacrifice to the Roman gods. When they refused, he had them tortured, and when they still would not worship the pagan gods, he had them beheaded. They were buried at Cyr in Syria, and later a great church was built there in their honor. Many years later, when the Emperor Justinian was very sick, he prayed to Sts. Damian and Cosmas for a cure. When his prayer was answered, he enlarged the town of Cyr and built a new church dedicated to the martyrs. As a result, devotion to them spread throughout the empire. Their names are listed in the First Eucharistic Prayer (the Roman Canon) among the martyrs to whom the whole Church prays. They died about 300. St. Cosmas is patron of doctors and druggists.

BLESSED DAMIEN DE VEUSTER
April 15

Blessed Damien, a native of Belgium, went as a missionary to Hawaii. Seeing the pitiful state of the lepers, he volunteered to take the love of God to the leper colony at Molokai. He remained there for the rest of his life and died of leprosy in 1889. When Pope John Paul II beatified him in 1995, he honored him as a "servant of humanity" and an inspiration to the world.

BLESSED DAMIEN DE VEUSTER

Daniel

(Hebrew: The Lord Is Judge)
Other Forms: Dan, Dane, Niel

Daniel
July 21

Daniel was one of the great prophets of the Old Testament. When
he was a youth, the king of Babylon attacked Jerusalem, overran it, and
took many of its people into captivity, among them Daniel. Because he
was handsome and bright, Daniel was trained in the king's household,
where he remained faithful to Jewish law despite many temptations.
He became very popular with the king, for whom he interpreted dreams,
including the fall of the kingdom to invaders. Under the conquering
King Darius, Daniel was thrown into a cage of lions to be eaten alive,
but when God saved his life, Darius ruled that all in his kingdom were
free to worship Daniel's God. Read all about Daniel in the Book of
Daniel in the Old Testament.

St. Daniel of Murano
March 31

St. Daniel of Murano was born in Germany. He went to Venice,
Italy, where he became a successful trader. A very holy man, he gave
his profits to the poor and lived in a monastery in Murano. He was
murdered by robbers in 1411.

David

(Hebrew: Beloved)
December 29

David was born in Bethlehem about a thousand years before Christ.
At that time Saul was king of Israel but he had lost the favor of God
because of disobedience. Therefore, under the inspiration of God, the
Prophet Samuel went to Bethlehem and anointed the boy David. Israel
was at war with the Philistines. One day his father, Jesse, sent David

DAVID

with food to his brothers who were in Saul's army. When David arrived in the camp, he found the Israelites fearful because the Philistines had a giant of a warrior against whom no man could stand. In fact, the giant Goliath only had to show himself and the Israelites fled. David told King Saul that he would meet Goliath. "You are only a boy," the king told him. "I have killed a lion and a bear that attacked my father's sheep," David replied. "The Lord will deliver me out of the hands of this Philistine." David went to meet Goliath with only a slingshot because the armor given him was too big and the sword too heavy. The giant came at the boy with sword upraised but David took his slingshot and hit Goliath between the eyes with a stone, knocking him to the ground, then took Goliath's sword and cut off the giant's head. David was made a member of the king's household because of his bravery, and he entertained Saul by playing the harp. After Saul died in battle, Samuel anointed David as king. As king, David made Jerusalem his capital, and brought the Ark of the Covenant there. He wrote beautiful psalms (songs) to God, which can be found in the Bible's Book of Psalms. David's own story can be read in the First and Second Book of Samuel. David's son Solomon succeeded his father to the throne and built the first great Temple to God. Solomon, like his father, was a great and wise king.

Other saints with this name:

ST. DAVID THE HERMIT (MESOPOTAMIA)
June 26

ST. DAVID OF RUSSIA
July 24

ST. DAVID OF SCOTLAND
May 24

DENIS

(Greek: God of Nyassa)
Other Forms: Dean, Dennis, Deno, Dion, Dionysius, Sidney, Sydney

ST. DENIS
October 9

St. Denis, bishop and martyr, is the patron saint of France. According to St. Martin of Tours, Denis was made the head of a mission band and sent from Rome to Gaul to preach the Gospel. He worked in the district of what is now Paris and is considered to be the first bishop of that city. Because of his missionary work, Denis, along with two companions, was put to death there about the year 250.

St. Paul arrived in Athens about the year 50. He preached the Gospel in the synagogue there without much success and also appeared in the marketplace to talk about Jesus. Athens at this time was full of idols of gods from everywhere. Some philosophers invited Paul to the Areopagus to speak to them, and there he delivered his famous Sermon on the Unknown God (Acts 17:22-31). The sermon did not make many converts, but a few did join the Church. Among them was Denis the Areopagite. There is a tradition which says Denis became bishop of Athens and later died a martyr. He is invoked against headaches.

DEVINICUS

(Celtic: Poet)
November 13
Another Form: Devin

St. Devinicus was a sixth-century Scottish missionary and bishop.

DOMINIC

(Latin: I Belong to the Lord)
August 8
Other Forms: Domenico, Domingo, Dominick

St. Dominic de Guzman was born in Spain in 1170. He studied theology there, and after he became a priest he worked closely with the bishop of Osma. In 1205, he and his bishop went to Rome, where Pope Innocent III spoke to them about his concern over the Albigensian heresy. St. Dominic decided to work to convert these heretics. He gathered some followers, who were called "preachers," and sent them out barefoot and practicing penance to preach the true faith and to expose the mistakes of the Albigenses. Ten years later this group, which had grown rapidly, was approved as an order of the Church, the Order of Preachers (Dominicans). St. Dominic urged his followers to study "on journeys, at home, by day and night." Dominicans soon became the leading teachers in Europe. St. Dominic also founded a convent of women who were to become the Dominican Sisters. He died in Italy in 1221.

Other saints with this name:

St. Dominic Loneatus (Italy)
October 14

St. Dominic Savio (Italy)
March 9

St. Dominic

DONALD

(Celtic: Dark Stranger)
July 15
Other Forms: Don, Donal, Donnell

St. Donald lived in Forfar, Scotland, in the eighth century. Not very much is known about him other than that he was a husband and father who urged his family to love and serve God. His nine daughters all became nuns and formed their own small community.

EDMUND

(Old English: Happy Protection)
November 16
Other Forms: Edmond, Eamon, Ned, Edmundo

St. Edmund was born into a very religious family at Abingdon, England. His mother wore a hairshirt and practiced strict penances. His father, Robert Rich, a successful merchant, entered a monastery. Edmund went to Europe to study and was in Paris teaching literature when he received word that his mother was dying. He returned home and after her death assumed responsibility for the family. He became a distinguished professor of sciences at Oxford University. After his sisters entered a convent, Edmund decided to become a priest. Following his ordination, he again became a professor at Oxford, this time teaching theology. He was appointed archbishop of Canterbury, and his honesty and desire to protect the rights of the Church brought him the enmity of King Henry III. Other bishops and priests sided with the king against the archbishop. Finally, Edmund was forced to withdraw from England, going in 1240 to France, where he died the same year.

Other saints with this name:

ST. EDMUND THE KING (ENGLAND)
November 20

ST. EDMUND CAMPION (ENGLAND)
October 25

EDWARD

(Old English: Rich Guardian)
October 13
Other Forms: Edoardo, Edouard, Eduard, Eduardo, Ned

St. Edward the Confessor was king of England for twenty-three years. He was born near Oxford about 1004. He succeeded to the throne of King Canute the Great, a Danish conqueror. Noted for his goodness and justice, Edward was a very popular king. He preferred to use wisdom rather than war to solve problems. He lowered taxes and made wise laws. He died January 5, 1066, and was succeeded by William the Conqueror.

Another saint by this name:

ST. EDWARD THE MARTYR (ENGLAND)
March 18

EDWIN

(Old English: Rich Friend)
October 12

St. Edwin was the king of Northumbria (England) who married St. Ethelburga. He was a pagan at the time of his wedding, but his wife's chaplain, St. Paulinus, converted him, and from then on he sought the conversion of his subjects. He fell in battle against a pagan king from Wales in 633.

ELIAS

(Hebrew: The Lord Is God)
July 20
Other Forms: Eli, Elijah

St. Elias is a popular saint of the Eastern churches. He is one of the major prophets of the Old Testament who lived in the eighth century before Christ. His story is in the Books of Kings. Newer translations of the Bible refer to him as Elijah. According to the Second Book of Kings (Chapter 2), Elijah was taken up to heaven in a flaming chariot traveling in a whirlwind.

EMIL

(Latin: Excelling)
May 28
Other Forms: Emile, Emilian, Emilion, Ernilius, Emlyn

St. Emil was a Christian soldier stationed in Romania. Because he overthrew some pagan altars, he was arrested and buried alive at Drisna. He died in 362.

Other saints with this name:

ST. EMILIAN OF NANTES (FRANCE)
June 27

ST. EMIL OF REDON (FRANCE)
October 11

EMMANUEL

(Hebrew: God With Us)
March 26
Other Forms: Emanuel, Immanuel, Manolo, Manuel

Emmanuel is a name given to Jesus Christ. The Prophet Isaiah used it to refer to the expected Messiah. Most people who are given this name are so named in honor of Jesus. St. Emmanuel was a martyr under Diocletian in Asia Minor. Nothing else is known of him.

Another saint with this name:

BLESSED EMMANUEL RUIZ (SPAIN)
July 10

ERIC

(Norse: Ever-Ruler)
May 18
Other Forms: Erich, Erik

St. Eric was elected king of Sweden in 1150. He led a holy life and was an inspiration to his people. His banner is held as a symbol of Swedish freedom, much as that of St. George in England. He died in battle in 1160 or 1161. This name is the Norse for Henry.

ERNEST

(Greek: Serious)
November 7
Other Forms: Ernesto, Ernst

St. Ernest was a Benedictine abbot of South Germany. He joined one of the Crusades and remained behind to preach the Gospel in Palestine. He eventually made his way to Arabia where he was seized by Muslims and put to death at Mecca in 1148.

EUGENE

(Greek: Well Born)
July 8
Other Forms: Eugenio, Yevgeny, Gene, Gino

St. Eugene was the bishop of Carthage in Africa at a time when the area was controlled by the Vandals, who favored the Arian heresy. Eugene's zeal and wisdom brought many Arians back into the Church. This alarmed the Arian bishops, and they appealed to King Huneric, who deported five thousand Christians to the land of the Moors and forbade Eugene to act as bishop. Eugene was sent into exile where he remained until the death of Huneric. Under the new king, Eugene was allowed to return to Carthage and reopen the Catholic churches. However, when this king died, his successor, Aleric II, was an Arian and deported Eugene to France, where he died in 505.

Other saints with this name:

St. Eugene of Paris (France)
November 15

Pope St. Eugene (Italy)
June 2

St. Eugene de Mazenod
December 3

Eustace

(Greek: Fruitful)
September 20

St. Eustace was a Roman officer who was a Christian. He, along with his wife and two sons, was arrested during the persecution of Hadrian (118 A.D.). Refusing to give up their faith, they were put to death. Their relics were kept in a church in Rome and later transferred to France where they were destroyed in 1567 by the anti-Catholic Huguenots.

Fabian

(Latin: Prosperous Farmer)
January 20

St. Fabian was still a layman when he was elected pope in 236. He was a great leader who reformed the discipline of the Church. He is said to have originated the Holy Thursday rite of Consecration of the Holy Oils which the Church still follows. He beautified the monuments to the martyrs. He was arrested during the persecution of Decian and put to death in 250.

FAUSTINO

(Latin: Lucky, Fortunate)

BLESSED FAUSTINO MIGUEZ
October 25

Blessed Faustino was a Spanish Scalopian priest who founded the Daughters of the Divine Shepherdess. His life as priest, educator, medical researcher, and founder was dedicated to "seeking souls and leading them to God." He died at the age of ninety-four in 1925. At his beatification in 1998, Pope John Paul II praised Faustino as "the very image of Christ who welcomes, pardons, and gives life."

BLESSED FAUSTINO PEREZ-GARCIA
August 13

Blessed Faustino Perez-Garcia was one of the Claretian martyrs of Barbastro, Spain, beatified by Pope John Paul II in 1992. A theology student, twenty-five years old, he was the seminarian-leader of the group of martyrs. On August 13 while in prison, he drafted a moving farewell to the congregation, promising that he would begin the cry of "Long live Christ the King!" as they drove to their execution. He was as good as his word, but after he had shouted the opening cry, one of his executioners hit him on the head with the butt of his revolver, mortally wounding him. Even in this bloodied state, he was shot with the others on August 15, 1936. His body was later identified by the deep imprint that had broken his skull.

FELIX

(Latin: Happy)
November 20
Other Forms: Felician, Feliejo, Feliz

St. Felix was a hermit who for many years lived alone in a forest. One day a visitor came from Paris to see him. He was John of Matha, who also was to become a saint. John told Felix about a desire he had to work for the ransom of Christians who were being captured by Muslim pirates and taken across the Mediterranean Sea to Africa. Felix replied that he would also like to do this work. They decided that they would found a society in honor of the Blessed Trinity that would be devoted to the ransom of captives. Together they went to Rome to seek permission, which Pope Innocent Ill gave them. Thus the Trinitarian Order was born. They founded a monastery in Rome that John of Matha headed. St. Felix began another monastery in France, which he governed until his death about 1212.

Other saints with this name:

St. Felix of Cordova (Spain)
July 27

St. Felix of Metz (Germany)
February 21

St. Felix of Milan (Italy)
July 21

Ferdinand

(Teutonic: Adventurous)
May 30
Other Forms: Ferde, Fernand, Fernando, Hernando

St. Ferdinand (Ferdinand III) was the king of Castile in Spain. His father was king of León and his mother the daughter of the king of Castile. After the death of her father in 1217, Ferdinand was proclaimed king of that country. When his own father died, Ferdinand also became king of León and thus united the two kingdoms. Muslims controlled a great part of Spain, and Ferdinand went to war with them. He drove the Muslims out of Cordova, which they had held for five centuries, took back the kingdom of Murcia, and after a two-year siege entered Seville, one of Spain's most important cities. He thus began the end of the Muslim control of Spain. He died in 1252.

FIDELIS

(Latin: Faithful)
April 24
Another Form: Fidel

St. Fidelis of Sigmaringen was born Mark Ray in southern Germany in 1577. He became a lawyer and was known for giving his services to the poor. In 1612 he entered religious life, joining the Capuchin Fathers and taking the name by which he is now known. He was sent as a missionary to the Swiss Protestants. He made many converts but finally was stabbed to death by an armed gang on April 24, 1622.

FRANCIS

(Teutonic: Free)
Other Forms: Francesco, Francisco, Franco, Francois, Frank, Franz

ST. FRANCIS OF ASSISI
October 4

St. Francis of Assisi is one of the most popular saints in the Roman calendar, loved by Catholics and non-Catholics because of the beauty of his life. He was born in Assisi, Italy, the son of a rich merchant. His early years were ones of delinquency, engaging in pleasures and brawls, and even spending time in the jails of Perugia. It was there that divine grace touched him and he was reborn as a saint. He took the Gospel counsels literally and began a life of poverty and love. Barefoot, in rough clothes, he begged for a living, preaching poverty, peace, and a love for all of God's creation. He called the wonders of nature and the animals his brothers and sisters. He worked with his hands, cared for lepers and the sick, swept out churches, and built other churches with his own hands. Others attracted by his life joined him, and thus the Franciscan Order was born. Clare of Assisi sought him for spiritual guidance and under the inspiration of Francis she founded the Sisters of the Poor (Franciscan or Poor Clare Sisters). God gave a visible blessing to his work by bestowing on Francis the stigmata, or wounds of Christ. Worn out by his labors, Francis lay down on the earth at the

Portiuncula, a chapel he had built, and there welcomed death on October 4, 1226. Pope Benedict XV called him the "most perfect image of Christ" that ever lived.

ST. FRANCIS OF ASSISI

St. Franics Xavier

St. Francis Xavier
December 3

St. Francis Xavier is the patron of foreign missions. Born into a family of minor nobility, which had its seat in the Castle of Xavier in the Basque country of Spain, Francis was privately tutored. Because of his brilliance, he was sent to the University of Paris, then the leading university in Europe. Here he gave himself up to pleasures as well as study. Another student at the university, a retired artillery captain named Ignatius Loyola, used to say to him, "Francis, what does it profit a man to gain the whole world if it costs him his soul?" Ignatius converted Francis to the service of Christ, and together with some other companions they formed the Society of Jesus. For some years, Francis worked in Italy, and then he was assigned to preach the Gospel in the Far East. He left for India in 1542. He had extraordinary success, baptizing tens of thousands. Fellow missioners told of his many miracles, even raising the dead to life. He also had the gift of tongues — people heard him in their own languages. Later he worked in Japan, laying the foundations of Christianity there. He died on Sancian Island, alone and almost abandoned, in 1552, while trying to get into China, which he could see in the distance. Francis's favorite prayer was, *"Da mihi animas"* (Give me souls). He was the greatest missionary the modern Church has ever produced.

St. Francis De Sales
January 24

St. Francis de Sales was born in the Savoy area of France about 1566. His father wanted him to be a lawyer, so he became one, serving in the Senate of Savoy. However, his own wish was to become a priest, and this he did. He was very popular as a preacher and spiritual director. In 1603 he was appointed bishop of Geneva. He inspired Madame de Chantal to found the Order of Visitation Sisters. Two of his books of spirituality, *Introduction to a Devout Life* and *Treatise on the Love of God*, have become classics, and he is the patron of writers. He died in 1622, calling himself "a useless servant."

Other saints with this name:

St. Francis Borgia (Spain)
October 10

St. Francis Caracciolo (Italy)
June 4

St. Francis Solanus (Peru)
July 14

FREDERICK

(Teutonic: Peace-Ruler)
July 18
Other Forms: Federico, Fred, Frederic, Friedrich

St. Frederick was a grandson of the king of the Frisians who grew up in holiness and became a priest. He was named bishop of Utrecht (Holland) and worked to end paganism and idolatry in the region. He also reproved some members of the nobility for leading bad lives, thus making enemies. One of these enemies had him killed in 838.

GABRIEL

(Hebrew: God's Strength)
Another Form: Gabe

GABRIEL THE ARCHANGEL
September 29

Gabriel is one of the three angels whose name is given in the Bible. In the Book of Daniel, Gabriel appeared to the Prophet Daniel twice to explain a vision that the prophet had concerning the Messiah. In the New Testament, Gabriel appeared first to the priest Zachary while he was burning incense in the Temple. Gabriel told him that Zachary's wife, Elizabeth, was to have a son whom he should name John. Gabriel identified himself this way: "I am Gabriel, who stands in the presence of God. I was sent to speak to you and bring you this good news." Six months later Gabriel appeared to the Virgin Mary, greeting her, "Hail, full of grace, the Lord is with you." Then Gabriel told her that she too was to have a son and that he should be named Jesus, about whose greatness he prophesied. You can read the account in the first chapter of Luke.

ST. GABRIEL LALLEMAND
October 19

St. Gabriel Lallemand is a North American martyr. While preaching the Gospel to the Huron Indians in 1649, he was captured by the Iroquois Indians and put to death.

GEORGE

(Greek: Farmer)
April 23
Other Forms: Georges, Giorgio, Igor, Jorge, Jurgen

St. George suffered martyrdom in Palestine about the year 308. His popularity spread rapidly in both the Latin and Greek Churches. In England he received great devotion, and he became patron saint of that country, where his feast day was a holy day which the archbishop of Canterbury ordered should have the same solemnity as Christmas. King Edward founded the Knights of St. George, which still exist as the Knights of the Garter. The most famous legend about St. George is how he went off on horseback to Libya where slew a terrible dragon that was devouring sheep and maidens, killing it with one blow of his lance. He is also patron of Boy Scouts.

GERALD

(Teutonic: Spear Rule)
March 13
Other Forms: Geraldo, Garcia, Jerold, Jerry

St. Gerald was an Irish monk who became the abbot of Mayo. He led a very holy life, given to much prayer and fasting. He died about 722.

GERARD

(Teutonic: Strong Spear)
October 16
Other Forms: Gerhard, Gerado, Gerry, Girado, Girard

St. Gerard Majella was born in 1726, just south of Naples, Italy. As a boy he was made an apprentice to a tailor. He joined the newly founded Redemptorist Order as a lay brother. He was so holy that crowds followed him everywhere, trying to touch him and give him petitions. His superiors had to move him from monastery to monastery so that he would have some sort of normal religious life. He worked many miracles while alive. He died in 1755, while still a young man. He is patron of mothers in difficult births.

Another saint with this name:

St. Gerard of Csanad (Hungary)
September 24

Gervais

(Teutonic: Spear Servant)
June 15
Other Forms: Gervas, Gervase, Gervasius, Jarvis, Jervis

On June 19, 886, St. Ambrose discovered the bodies of two martyrs who had been buried at Milan. They were named Gervase and Protasius. Devotion to the martyrs spread rapidly through the West, although little else was known about them.

Gilbert

(Teutonic: Bright Pledge)
February 4

St. Gilbert was born in England during the reign of William the Conqueror. He was the son of a Norman officer who had served the king so well that he had been awarded the Manor of Sempringham. Although his father wanted him to be a soldier, Gilbert chose to go to the University of Paris to study. Returning with his master of arts, he opened a school at Sempringham to serve poor children. The bishop of Lincoln persuaded him to become a priest. After the death of his father, Gilbert used his inheritance to found two monasteries, one for nuns, the other for monks, called Gilbertines. Accused of helping the exiled archbishop of Canterbury, St. Thomas Becket, Gilbert was imprisoned for a time. He lived to be over a hundred and until his death in 1190 continued to serve the poor.

GODFREY

(Teutonic: God's Peace)
November 8
Other Forms: Geoffrey, Goffredo, Gottfried, Jeff, Jeffrey

When St. Godfrey was a boy in France he entered the monastery of St. Quentin. There he was educated, became a monk, and was elected abbot of Nogent. He became widely known for his wisdom and sanctity and was appointed bishop of Amiens. He was never happy as bishop, always wishing to live as a simple monk. He died in 1115, loved and respected by the people he served.

GREGORY

(Greek: Watchman)
Other Forms: Greg, Gregor, Gregoire, Gregorio

GREGORY THE GREAT
September 3

Pope St. Gregory the Great is called a Doctor (Teacher) of the Church. He is also patron of singers and scholars. Born into a well-to-do family, Gregory entered public service and became prefect (governor) of Rome. Then he resigned his position of power, and he used his wealth to found the Monastery of St. Andrew, to which he withdrew. After being papal ambassador to Byzantium, he was elected pope in 590. As pope he set about reforming the Church. He revised the liturgy, encouraged the growth of monasticism, sent missionaries to England and other European countries, established Gregorian chant music, revised the calendar, fought heresy, and developed the temporal powers of the papacy. He wrote many books on faith and morals. He died March 12, 604.

ST. GREGORY NAZIANZEN
January 2

A close friend and cooperator with St. Basil the Great in combatting Arianism and in developing monasticism, St. Gregory was born at

Nazianzus in Asia Minor in 330. He became the Bishop of Constantinople and presided over the Second Ecumenical Council. He is called The Theologian because of his writings on the Trinity and his spiritual poetry. Many of his sermons and letters still exist and are a valuable record of theological thought in the early Church. He died about 389.

St. Gregory the Wonder Worker
November 17

A Father of the Church, St. Gregory was called the Wonder Worker because of the many miracles he did in his lifetime. His miracles are said to have converted the city of Neocaesarea in Asia Minor where he was bishop. He was also a man of great virtue. He died about 272.

Other saints with this name:

St. Gregory of Tours (France)
November 17

St. Gregory Grassi (China)
July 7

Guy

(Old French: Guide)
September 12
Another Form: Guido

St. Guy was a poor youth who lived near Brussels, Belgium. For some years he was sacristan in the church at Lacken. He decided to make a pilgrimage to Jerusalem, no easy feat in those days. On the way back he passed through Rome, where he met the vicar of Anderlecht, who was leading a group of pilgrims to the Holy Land. Guy offered to serve as their guide. The group reached Jerusalem safely, but on the way back home plague struck the travelers, and all died except Guy. Sick and exhausted from the two journeys, Guy finally reached Anderlecht to tell of what had happened. There he died in 1012. He is invoked for the protection of dogs and against rabies. He is the patron of those with epilepsy.

Another saint with this name:

BLESSED GUY OF CORTONA (ITALY)
June 12

GYAVIRA

June 3

Gyavira was one of the young Christian pages among the martyrs of Uganda. In prison before his execution, he forgave another of the pages who had hurt him during a quarrel. An example for peacemakers, he was burned to death on June 3, 1886, without ceasing to pray.

HAROLD

(Danish: Strong Warrior)
November 1
Another Form: Harry

St. Harold was the first Christian king of Denmark. He sought to convert his people to Christianity and was put to death by pagan idolaters who had revolted because of his religion. He died in 980.

HARVEY

(Teutonic: Warrior)
June 17
Another Form: Herve

St. Harvey, or Herve, as he is called in France, is a popular saint in Brittany. He was born blind, and his mother entrusted his education to an uncle who had a small monastic school. St. Harvey decided to become a monk and eventually was put in charge of his uncle's monastery. As the monastery grew, St. Harvey led a group of monks and scholars to found a new monastery. He became well known for his preaching and even in his lifetime was called a saint by the people. He died about 550.

HENRY

(Teutonic: Home Ruler)
July 15
Other Forms: Emeric, Enrico, Hank, Heinrich, Henri, Rico

St. Henry the Emperor was born in Bavaria, Germany, in 973. He succeeded his father as duke of Bavaria, and because of his outstanding qualities he was elected emperor of the Holy Roman Empire, which included most of Germany, Austria, Switzerland, Belgium, Holland, and the north of Italy. He was consecrated emperor at Mainz, June 16, 1007. He is called "the most Christian prince" because of his work for the Church. Henry brought about necessary reforms, protected the papacy, encouraged missionary activity, and founded monasteries and dioceses. In his own life he gave great Christian example, practicing the Gospel virtues.

Another saint with this name:

ST. HENRY SUSO (GERMANY)
January 23

HERBERT

(Teutonic: Shining Warrior)
March 20
Other Forms: Bert, Herb

St. Herbert was an English hermit who was a close friend of the great monk St. Cuthbert. He lived on an island in Lake Derwentwater where he practiced all sorts of penances and fasting. He often prayed that he would die on the same day as his friend Cuthbert. This grace was granted him when both men died on the same day in 687.

HERMAN

(Teutonic: Soldier)

April 7

Other Forms: Armand, Armando, Ernan, Germain, German, Hermann, Herme, Hernando

Blessed Herman Joseph is known for his holy life and for his ability to read the hearts of people who came to him for spiritual advice. He was born in Cologne, Germany, and as a youth entered the Premonstratensian Order to study for the priesthood. He was a man of much prayer, and he spent long hours in chapel. He had great devotion to the Blessed Virgin and is reputed to have had visions and conversations with her. Despite the harshness he imposed upon himself, he lived to be almost a hundred. He died in 1241.

HILARION

(Latin: Merry)

Other Forms: Hilaire, Hilary

ST. HILARION

October 21

Born of pagan parents in Egypt, Hilarion was converted and baptized when he was fifteen years old. During a journey into the desert, he came upon St. Anthony, the Hermit of the Desert. He was so impressed by the life of this holy man, that when he returned to Alexandria, he gave his possessions to the poor and went to live on a marshy island. His holy life attracted other monks who came to him for advice, as well as many pilgrims. So many people were coming to him that he decided to move away to find solitude. He went to Greece, Dalmatia, and Sicily, each time being forced to move on because of the crowds that followed him. He finally settled on a remote mountain peak in Cyprus where he worshipped God until he died about 372.

St. Hilary of Poitiers
January 13

St. Hilary is a Doctor (Teacher) of the Church. He was born of a rich pagan family and was not converted to Christianity until he was thirty-five years old. He was elected bishop of Poitiers; and spent the rest of his life opposing the Arian heresy, which denied the truth of the Trinity. Because of his zeal, St. Hilary was exiled for four years by the Emperor Constantine. He is credited with ridding Gaul of Arianism. He wrote many works on Scripture and the Catholic faith. He died in 367, and is invoked for protection against snakes.

HUGH

(Teutonic: Bright Mind)
November 3
Another Form: Umberto

St. Hubert is a popular saint of the Middle Ages, invoked against rabies and for the protection of dogs. He is patron of hunters, foresters, furriers, and makers of precision instruments. In 705 he became bishop of Tongres, in Belgium, and was very popular. He traveled widely through his big diocese, sometimes on horseback and sometimes by boat. He replaced shrines to idols with Christian sanctuaries. He was particularly devoted to prisoners and is said to have smuggled food to them through the windows of their cells. He died near Brussels, Belgium, in 727.

HUGH

(Teutonic: Thought)
April 1
Other Forms: Hughes, Hugo, Ugo

St. Hugh is a man who wanted to be a monk but instead had to be a bishop. He was appointed to the post of bishop of Grenoble in 1080. He withdrew to a monastery, but the pope told him to go back to his job. About six years after Hugh became bishop, St. Bruno and six companions came to Grenoble looking for a hermitage. Hugh led them to the wildest and remotest place in his diocese, and there the famous abbey of Grand Chartreuse was founded, to which Hugh came as often as he could to share the life of the monks. Hugh never used a horse, traveling his diocese by foot. He sold his possessions to give money to the poor. A popular preacher, he died in 1131.

St. Ignatius Loyola

IGNATIUS

(Greek: Fiery)
Other Forms: Ignace, Ignacio, Ignazio, Inigo, Nacho

ST. IGNATIUS OF ANTIOCH
October 17

St. Ignatius was the second bishop of Antioch, succeeding St. Peter. In the persecution of Emperor Trajan St. Ignatius was arrested and taken to Rome to be put to death, enduring many trials on the way. During the journey he wrote seven letters to the various churches which are valuable records of his time and show the development of theology in the early Church. In Rome he was taken to the Colosseum, where he was thrown to wild beasts. Two lions devoured him.

ST. IGNATIUS LOYOLA
July 31

St. Ignatius was born in Loyola, Spain, in 1491. He joined the army and became a captain of artillery. In the siege of Pamplona, he was gravely wounded when a cannonball struck his leg. Taken to the Castle of Loyola for his recovery, he could find only two books to help him pass the time. One was a life of Christ and the other the lives of saints. After reading these books, he resolved he would serve Christ and His Mother as faithfully as he had served the queen. He went to the University of Paris to study to become a priest. There he gathered about him a small group of young men whom he formed into the Society of Jesus (the Jesuits). The Society grew with speed and importance. He died in Rome in 1556.

ISAAC

(Hebrew: He Laughs)
October 19

St. Isaac Jogues was born in Orleans, France. He became a Jesuit and after ordination was sent to Canada to do mission work. He was captured in New York State by the Mohawk Indians of the Iroquois tribe. He was taken to Auriesville, New York, where he was tortured. During the torture, several of his fingers were chewed off by women. St. Isaac managed to escape, and he made his way down the Hudson River to New York. He returned to France to regain his health, but came back to America to preach to the Indians. While seeking a way to preach to the Mohawks, he was again captured in New York State and this time was put to death.

ISIDORE

(Greek: Strong Gift)
May 10
Other Forms: Dore, Dorian, Dory

St. Isidore the Farmer is the patron saint of Madrid, Spain. Born into a poor family, he spent his life as a workman and became a saint through his love of God and the sanctification of daily tasks. He died in 1170, and his body was later found to be incorrupt. Because the ordinary Spanish people could identify with him, Isidore became a very popular saint. Spanish colonists brought this devotion to the New World, and he became popular among the Indians.

BLESSED ISIDORE BAKANJA
August 12

Isidore Bakanja was a young Zairois catechist who was beaten to death in hatred of the faith in 1909. A member of the Boangi tribe, Isidore was working as a servant boy to a Belgian colonizer when another colonizer ordered him to remove his scapular, calling him an "animal of stupid priests." To Isidore, his scapular and his rosary were badges of his faith. A few days later when the colonizer noticed that Isidore had not removed the offending scapular, he yanked the scapular from Isidore's neck and threw it to the dogs. He then had him beaten with more than two hundred lashes of an elephant-hide strap studded with nails. During the beating, the colonizer himself kicked Isidore fiercely. At last the bloody and wounded catechist was carried to a hut and left for dead. Isidore was found and treated by a Belgian inspector, but his

BLESSED ISIDORE BAKANJA

wounds were too infected to heal. After months of agony as an invalid, the catechist miraculously stood up, prayed the Rosary, then lay back down and died quietly. He was beatified, a martyr for the scapular, in 1994.

Other saints with this name:

St. Isidore of Seville (Spain)
April 4

St. Isidore of Egypt
January 15

Ives

(Teutonic: Archer)
May 19
Other Forms: Ivar, Iver, Ivo, Ivor, Yves

St. Ives was born in the Breton region of France and became a man of many careers. He was a priest, pastor, lawyer, and judge. He had a great love of St. Francis of Assisi and tried to imitate him in his life. He wore coarse clothing, gave alms to the poor and unfortunate, and supported orphans by taking them into his own home. He died in 1303.

James

(English form of Jacob, Hebrew: Supplanter)
Other Forms: Diego, Iago, Jacob, Jacques, Jaime, Jake, Jim, Santiago, Seamas, Shamus, Yakov

St. James, the Brother of St. John
July 25

St. James the Apostle, brother of St. John, is sometimes called James the Greater to distinguish him from another Apostle by the same name (James the Less). He was a fisherman and a son of Zebedee. He and his brother John were mending nets with their father when Jesus called upon them to follow Him. Because of the fiery nature of these two brothers, Jesus called them "Sons of Thunder." James, along with John and Peter, was allowed to see the Transfiguration of Jesus. One day his mother went to Jesus to ask that her sons receive special honor in Jesus' kingdom. He told her that they would have to suffer with Him and that they would have to earn any honors. According to legend, St. James went to Spain after the death of Jesus and preached the Gospel. Called back to Jerusalem, he returned with some disciples. There he was arrested by Herod Agrippa and was beheaded. His disciples took his bones back to Spain, burying them in Galicia, where a great shrine was built to him at Compostela which has attracted millions of pilgrims through the centuries. He is the patron of Spain, and the Muslims were driven out under the banner of Santiago (San Iago, or St. James). Many places have been named in his honor, such as Santiago, Chile. He was the first Apostle martyred.

St. James, the Relative of the Lord
May 3

St. James, sometimes called the Less, was the son of Alphaeus, a cousin of St. Jude, and a relative of Jesus probably called the Less because Jesus called him after the other James, not because he was any less important. He wrote an epistle which can be found in the New Testament. He became the first bishop of Jerusalem and presided over the Church there while the other Apostles went forth preaching the Gospel. He is said to have led a prayerful life of penance. In the year 62 he was arrested by Jewish officials. He was thrown from the Temple roof. Badly injured but not quite dead, he was then stoned to death.

Jason

(Hebrew: God Is My Savior; Greek: One Who Cures)
December 3

Jason was the son of Claudius, a Roman tribune. He became a convert after seeing the bravery of St. Chrysanthus under torture. Jason, his father, his brother, and his father's soldiers were drowned. His mother died for her faith in prison. They were martyred in the year 283.

79

JEREMIAS

(Hebrew: Exalted of the Lord)
May 1
Other Forms: Geremia, Jeremy, Jeremiah

Jeremias was one of the major prophets of the Old Testament.

ST. JEROME

JEREMY

February 16
Other Forms: Jeremiah, Jeremias

St. Jeremy was a martyr killed in Palestine in the fourth century.

JEROME

(Greek: Holy Name)
September 30
Other Forms: Geronimo, Hieronymus, Jerry

St. Jerome is a Doctor (Teacher) of the Church. He was born in Dalmatia and went to Rome to study. There he was baptized. For a time he lived the life of a monk. After he was ordained as priest, he gave himself up to scholarship and study of Scripture. Later Jerome returned to Rome and became secretary for Pope Damasus, who ordered him to prepare a Latin translation of the Bible. Jerome went to Bethlehem and for the next thirty years worked to produce the Latin Vulgate translation which has been in use to our own times. He also wrote on many theological and scriptural subjects. Jerome died in Bethlehem in 420. He is a patron of students.

Another saint by this name:

ST. JEROME EMILIANI (ITALY)
February 8

JESUS

(Hebrew: God Will Help)

Through a special feeling of reverence, most Christian nations have traditionally refrained from giving their children the given name of Our Lord. In Spanish-speaking countries, however, the name is customary and common. Any feast of Christ may be used as a name day.

Blessed Jesus was a professed lay brother in the Marianist congregation during the turbulent Spanish Revolution. Seeing the horrors of the persecution of religion, he practiced penitential acts. He was arrested and executed on September 25, 1936, along with Blessed Juan Pedro, Pablo Maria, and two priests. Their bodies were thrown into a well.

JOACHIM

(Hebrew: God Prepares)
July 26
Another Form: Joaquin

Joachim is the name given to the father of the Blessed Virgin Mary. Devotion to the parents of Mary is an ancient one in the Eastern Churches and more recently in the West.

JOEL

(Hebrew: The Coming Down of God)
July 13

St. Joel was one of the twelve minor prophets of the Old Testament, and his prophecy may be read there. He foretells of the evils that were to fall upon the Jews but promises that God will send them a teacher of justice (Jesus Christ) and the Holy Spirit. He prophesied around the year 780 B.C.

JOHN

(Hebrew: God Has Mercy)
Other Forms: Baptiste, Evan, Gian, Giovanni, Hans, Ian, Ivan, Jack, Jan, Johann, Johannes, Jon, Jonathan, Jonathon, Juan, Sean, Shane, Shaun, Shawn

ST. JOHN THE BAPTIST
June 24, August 29

John the Baptist was the son of Zechariah, a temple priest, and Elizabeth, a cousin of Mary, the Mother of Jesus Christ. His birth was surrounded by miraculous happenings (see the Gospel of Luke, chapter one). His purpose in life was to prepare the way for Jesus by preaching penance. As a young man, he retired to the desert to live, subsisting on locusts and wild honey. When Jesus came to John to be baptized, John called Jesus "the Lamb of God." Some of John's disciples left him to follow Jesus. Not long after, he was arrested by Herod and then beheaded through the trickery of Salome (see the Gospel of St. Mark, chapter six). Jesus said of him: "Among those born of women, none is greater than John."

ST. JOHN THE BAPTIST

St. John the Apostle and Evangelist
December 27

St. John, Apostle and Evangelist, was a disciple of St. John the Baptist when he first met Jesus. Later while he was repairing nets at the Sea of Galilee with his brother James, the two of them were invited by the Master to follow Him as His disciples. He became very beloved to Jesus, was with Him at the Transfiguration, and next to Him at the Last Supper. On the Cross Jesus gave His mother, Mary, to the safekeeping of John. After the death of Jesus, John and Peter worked together closely. Later John was arrested and exiled. It was reported that he was plunged into boiling oil but miraculously saved. He went to Asia Minor to live and teach, and wrote his Gospel and Epistles and the Book of Revelation. He died a very old man, still teaching the love of Jesus.

St. John Bosco
January 31

As a young priest in Italy in the mid-1800s, Don Bosco began a work with youth that survives today in the Salesian Order and its women's branch, the Daughters of Mary Help of Christians. The special charism of this order lies in the joy they find in serving God by helping the young to help themselves. Italy, during Bosco's lifetime, was anticlerical so he was much criticized and often attacked. A large gray dog that seemed to appear from nowhere and disappear in the same manner often accompanied him on his night calls and more than once saved him from people intent on harming him. His life was characterized by patience and he was gifted with vivid dreams, which showed him the correct actions to take. He died in 1888. Of this saintly founder Pope Pius XI said, "In his life the supernatural almost became natural and the extraordinary, ordinary." St. John Bosco's innate joy and his patience make him an excellent advocate for youth.

Blessed Juan Diego
December 9

Juan Diego is the Christian Baptismal name given to Cuauhtlatohuac, an Aztec Indian of Mexico. His Aztec name means "the eagle who speaks."

In 1531 he was given the extraordinary grace of a vision of the Blessed Virgin Mary, who left the imprint of her picture on his tilma (cloak). This image has been revered over the centuries under the name of Our Lady of Guadalupe. Pope John Paul II beatified Juan Diego by confirming his cult on May 6, 1990, in Mexico City.

There are more saints with the name of John than with any other name. Some of them are:

St. John Capistrano (Italy)
March 28

St. John Chrysostom (Syria)
September 13

St. John de Brébeuf (United States)
October 19

St. John Gabriel Perboyre (France/China)
November 7

St. John Neumann (United States)
January 5

St. John of the Cross (Spain)
December 14

St. John of God (Portugal)
March 8

Joseph

(Hebrew: Increase)
March 19
Other Forms: Giuseppe, Joe, Jose, Josef

St. Joseph was the husband of the Blessed Virgin Mary and foster father of Our Lord Jesus Christ. He was a carpenter in the town of

ST. JOSEPH

Nazareth. He was a descendant of the line of King David, and the New Testament calls him "a just man." He was advised in a dream about the child Mary was to have, and he took her with him when he went to Bethlehem to enroll in a census that was being taken. There Jesus was born in a stable because all the inns were crowded. Joseph was warned in a dream to flee with Mary and the child to Egypt to escape the jealousy of Herod. After a period of exile there, he returned with Jesus and Mary to Nazareth. Each year it was his custom to take Jesus and Mary to Jerusalem for the Passover. They made this journey when Jesus was twelve years old, and on the way back to

Nazareth they missed the boy, each having thought that He was with others. They went back to Jerusalem, and after three days they found Jesus teaching in the Temple. Sometime after this Joseph died in Nazareth. The Church holds St. Joseph in great honor because of his care for Jesus and his love for Mary. He is patron of carpenters and laborers and is prayed to for a good death.

St. Joseph Moscatti
November 16

St. Joseph Moscatti was a physician of Naples, Italy, who understood the way of service and sanctification in everyday life. A man of intense prayer, he considered his chapel a classroom or clinic. He labored among the poor until his death on April 12, 1927. He was canonized in 1987.

Other saints with this name:

St. Joseph Calasanz (Spain)
August 25

St. Joseph Benedict Cottolengo (Italy)
April 30

St. Joseph Cupertino (Italy)
September 18

Jude

(Hebrew: Praised)
October 28

St. Jude is one of the Twelve Apostles. He was the son of James, not otherwise identified. St. Mark gives him also the name of Thaddeus. At the Last Supper he was the one who asked Jesus why He had revealed Himself only to the disciples and not to the whole world. According to tradition he preached the Gospel in Persia with St. Simon and was martyred there. He is invoked for desperate cases.

JULIUS

(Latin: Soft Beard)
April 12
Other Forms: Giles, Giulio, Jules, Julian, Julio

Pope St. Julius was a Roman citizen who was elected in 337. His papacy was filled with many trials because of heretics. He was a defender of St. Athanasius, who had been driven from his see in Alexandria because of his fight against the Arian heretics. Pope Julian died in 352 and was buried in the catacomb of St. Callixtus.

Another saint with this name:

ST. JULIAN OF TOLEDO (SPAIN)
March 8

JUSTIN

(Latin: Just)
August 1

Justin was a young Christian boy in France who died as a martyr. One day he and his father were making a trip from Paris to Amiens when a band of men searching for Christians came upon them. Justin's father escaped and hid, but Justin was caught. Despite being beaten, he refused to tell the men in what direction his father had gone, and he likewise refused to deny that he was a Christian. The men killed the boy when they could get nothing from him. He died about 288.

KENNETH

(Celtic: Handsome)
October 1
Other Forms: Ken, Canice, Canute, Kent, Knute

St. Kenneth is the patron of Kilkenny, Ireland, and a friend and follower of St. Columba. He left St. Columba and the monastery of Iona and settled in the diocese of Ossory, where he founded the church at Kilkenny. He died in the year 600.

KEVIN

(Gaelic: Handsome)
June 3

St. Kevin is one of the patrons of Dublin, Ireland. He is said to have been of royal descent. He was educated by Irish monks, became a priest, and decided to be a hermit. His holiness and cures of the sick brought him many disciples, and he founded the Abbey of Glendalough, which became a place of pilgrimage. He died in 618.

KIERAN

(Gaelic: Black)
March 5

St. Kieran was a contemporary of St. Patrick and is called by the Irish their first native-born saint. Both Ossory and Cork claim to be his birthplace. He received an elementary education in Christianity and then went to Rome to be more fully instructed. According to ancient accounts, it was on this trip that he first met St. Patrick. When Patrick came to Ireland, St. Kieran was one of the twelve men he appointed bishops to assist him. St. Kieran is venerated as the first bishop of Ossory. He died about 530.

KILLIAN

(Celtic: Church)
July 8
Another Form: Kilian

St. Killian was an Irish missioner who went to preach the Gospel in Thuringia, Germany, along with St. Colman. They were both put to death there for their efforts about 689.

KIZITO

(Luganda: Born After Twins)
June 3

At the age of fourteen, Kizito was the youngest of the Uganda martyrs. A page in the court of the debauched king of Buganda, Kizito was baptized by St. Charles Lwanga the night before he was imprisoned. Seeing that he seemed frightened, St. Charles promised to hold

ST. LAWRENCE

his hand as they walked to their death. All the witnesses testified that Kizito walked happily to his execution, laughing and singing, radiant with Christian joy. He was burned to death on June 3, 1886, never ceasing to pray as the flames took his life.

LADISLAS

(Slavic: Ruling Well)
June 27
Other Forms: Ladislaus, Lance, Lancelot, Lazlo, Vladislas

St. Ladislas is a great figure in Hungarian history. He succeeded to the throne in 1077 and had to put down rebellions, drive the Tartars back to Russia, and fight the Serbs and Bulgars. He acted always in the best interests of his people. A huge man, he was very popular with the soldiers he led into battle. He was a man of great wisdom, and when it came time for the West to choose a leader for the First Crusade, the French, English, and Spanish unanimously selected Ladislas. He accepted, but he died in 1095 before he could take the expedition to the Holy Land. He was a man of great virtue who tried always to do the will of God.

LAWRENCE

(Latin: Laurel)
August 10
Other Forms: Larry, Lars, Laurel, Lauren, Laurence, Laurenz, Lauritz, Loren, Lorenzo

St. Lawrence was a deacon who was martyred, and devotion to him became widespread in Europe. Lawrence was an assistant to Pope Sixtus II. In 258, Emperor Valerian issued an edict against Christians which declared that all Christians would be put to death and their property confiscated. One of the first arrested was Pope Sixtus. Lawrence then was brought before the prefect of Rome and ordered to deliver up all the wealth of the Church. He asked for a delay and used the time to give alms to the poor. The next day he returned to the prefect, followed by beggars. "Here is the wealth of the Church," Lawrence told the prefect. Angered at having been tricked, the prefect ordered that Lawrence should be roasted to death over a slow fire. St. Ambrose tells us that even in death Lawrence kept his humor. "I'm well done on this side," he told his tormentors. "Turn me over to the other." He died praying for the city of Rome. He is patron of cooks and invoked against fire.

Other saints with this name;

St. Lawrence of Brindisi (Italy)
July 21

St. Lawrence Justinian (Italy)
September 6

Leo

(Latin: Lion)
November 10
Other Forms: Lee, Leon, Lon, Leov, Lionel

Pope St. Leo the Great ruled the Church in one of its greatest periods of upheaval. A native of Rome, he became pope in 440. The Church at the time was afflicted by many heresies, including Pelagianism, Nestorianism, Manichaeanism. At the same time, the Roman Empire was being attacked by Huns, Goths, Visigoths, and Vandals. On one occasion, St. Leo rode out to meet Attila the Hun and persuaded him not to advance on Rome. During this confusing period, St. Leo held the Church together, strengthened the authority of the papacy and at the same time lived a life of holiness. He died in 461.

Leonard

(Teutonic: Lionhearted)
November 6
Other Forms: Leonardo, Leonhard

St. Leonard is the patron of prisoners. He was a Frankish lord who fought alongside King Clovis. With Clovis he was baptized at Rheims in 496. Clovis wished to make him a bishop, but Leonard refused. He did not wish even to be a priest, although he allowed himself to be ordained a deacon. He asked Clovis for permission to visit the prisons and to free those that he found deserving. Clovis granted his wish, and he spent most of the remainder of his life working among captives and prisoners. He built a sanctuary in a forest and there gathered disciples around him, many of them former prisoners. He died about 599.

LEOPOLD

(German: People's Prince)
November 15
Other Forms: Leo, Leopoldo, Lupo

To St. Leopold's name is usually added the phrase "The Pious," because of his holy life. He was born into the Austrian nobility. He was the grandson of Emperor Henry III; one of his sons became Emperor Conrad, and another was the father of the famous Frederick Barbarossa. He was a brave general of the Austrian army who drove back Hungarian invaders. He died in 1136, respected and loved by the people.

LOUIS

(Teutonic: Famous Warrior)
August 25
Other Forms: Alois, Aloysius, Lewis, Ludovico, Ludwig, Luigi, Luis

St. Louis, King of France, was the leader of the seventh and eighth Crusades. He became king when only eleven years old and took the name of Louis IX. He had six sons and five daughters. Falling sick, Louis vowed he would lead a crusade to the Holy Land if he recovered. He recovered, and he organized an army which he led to Egypt in 1246. After some early successes, St. Louis was captured by the Muslims. He gave back one of the places he had captured as ransom and was allowed to go on to Jerusalem. He returned to France in 1254 and set about developing his kingdom, building hospitals, Sainte Chapelle, and starting the Sorbonne University. He had the respect of all the kings of

Europe and was considered a saint by the people. St. Louis became a blacksmith to identify with the working people. He died in 1270 while preparing to attack Tunis on his last crusade. His remains were brought back to Paris and buried in the Church of St. Denis He is patron of builders and other workers.

LUKE

(Greek: Light)
October 18
Other Forms: Luc, Luca, Lucas, Lucian, Luciano, Lucio, Lucius

St. Luke was the only evangelist who was not a Jew. He belonged to the Greek world, and St. Paul refers to him as "beloved Luke, the physician." He was converted by St. Paul when Paul and Barnabas came to Antioch to preach Christianity. He became a scribe and companion to St. Paul and remained with the Apostle of the Gentiles throughout his captivity. St. Luke wrote the third Gospel, based on what St. Paul and others told him. He did make one journey to Jerusalem with Paul, and it is thought that while there he interviewed the Blessed Mother. His Gospel has much material not found in the other Gospels, particularly about the infancy of Christ. He also wrote The Acts of the Apostles, which tells of life in the early Church and of the work of Peter and Paul. There is no record of when he died, but some historians believe he died naturally in Rome. He is patron of doctors and artists.

MALACHY

(Hebrew: Messenger of the Lord)
November 2
Other Forms: Mal, Malachi

St. Malachy was born in Armagh, Ireland. He became a priest and then abbot at Connor. He was appointed archbishop of Armagh, but he gave way to a rival. A very holy man who suffered many trials and who is said to have worked miracles in his lifetime, he was respected by the people. On a trip to Rome, he visited the Abbey of Clairvaux in France, and there died in 1148 in the presence of his friend St. Bernard.

ST. MARTIN DE PORRES

MARK

(Latin: Of Mars)
April 25
Other Forms: Marc, Marcel, Marco, Marcus, Markus

St. Mark, sometimes referred to in the New Testament as John Mark, was a cousin of St. Barnabas and a native of Jerusalem. His mother, Mary, was a Christian, and her house was a meeting place for early Christians. Some think that it was in her house that the Last Supper was held. Some Scripture scholars identify Mark with the young man in his Gospel who ran away naked when Christ was arrested in the Garden. Others believe he was baptized by St. Peter, who calls him "his son." In the year 44, Mark joined Sts. Paul and Barnabas on a missionary journey to Cyprus and Asia Minor. Later he made another trip with Barnabas and still later was with Paul in Rome. It is believed that he gathered most of the material for his Gospel, which was the first one written, perhaps as early as 50, from St. Peter. Egyptian Copts claim St. Mark as the founder of the Church in Egypt. Tradition also says he died during the persecution of Trajan. He is patron of lawyers and is invoked against the loss of faith.

MARTIN

(Latin: Warlike)
Other Forms: Martino, Marty

ST. MARTIN DE PORRES
November 3

St. Martin was born in Lima, Peru, to a Spanish father and black mother. As a boy he learned the basics of medicine in an apprenticeship and then entered the Dominican monastery as a lay brother. He worked for the city's poor, begging for their needs and using his medical skills on their illnesses. He was given to fervent prayer and once prayed through an earthquake without noticing it. He had a particular devotion to the Holy Eucharist. Like St. Francis, he had a special way with animals, and he used to gather the mice each day to feed them. He is reputed to have worked many miracles in his life. He died in 1639.

ST. MARTIN OF TOURS
November 11

St. Martin of Tours was a soldier. When he was about twenty, he was baptized and left the army to serve St. Hilary of Poitiers. Later he retired to become a monk and helped found Ligugé, the most ancient monastery in the West. When in 371 the people of Tours were seeking

ST. MARTIN OF TOURS

a bishop, they elected Martin by acclamation. He was soon noted for his praying, preaching, and good works. He traveled widely through France, converting whole districts. Whenever he converted an area, he would leave behind monks and priests to build up the Church. When he died in 897, Martin was so popular that hundreds of villages were named after him and it is said that four thousand churches were dedicated to him in France alone. He is the patron of horsemen.

St. Matthew

MATTHEW

(Hebrew: The Lord's Gift)
Other Forms: Matt, Matteo, Matthaus, Matthias
St. Matthew
September 21

St. Matthew, Apostle and Evangelist, was a tax collector called Levi when Jesus invited him to become an Apostle. He was a native of Capernaum where Jesus did His early preaching. After the death of Jesus, he wrote his Gospel in Aramaic for the Palestinian Jews to show that Jesus was the promised Messiah. Tradition says that he preached the Gospel in the East and was martyred there.

St. Matthias
May 14

St. Matthias was the Apostle who was chosen to take the place of Judas. He had been a disciple of Jesus and had traveled about Palestine with the Master. After Jesus had ascended to heaven, the eleven Apostles met in Jerusalem to pick a successor to the traitor Judas. Two men were nominated, Justus and Matthias. A vote was taken and Matthias was elected. There are two traditions about St. Matthias. One is that he preached the Gospel in Ethiopia and was put to death there, another that he was martyred in Palestine. He is the patron of tailors and alcoholics.

MAURICE

(Greek: Dark)
September 22
Other Forms: Maur, Mauricio, Maurizio, Moritz, Morris

Maurice was an Egyptian, a member of Rome's Theban Legion. In 286 there was an uprising against Rome in Gaul. The Theban Legion, along with other troops, was sent from Italy over the Alps to put down the disturbance. Before going into battle, the commander ordered his troops to sacrifice to the gods. Maurice and some other Christian soldiers refused, and they were put to death.

Maximilian

(Latin: Greatest)
October 12
Other Forms: Massimiliano, Massimo, Maxim, Max

St. Maximilian was a native of the Austria-Germany area of Europe. After working as a lay missioner, he became a priest and was later appointed bishop of Lorsch. While visiting his territory he was arrested for being a Christian. He was ordered to offer sacrifice to the god Mars. When he refused, he was put to death about 281.

St. Maximilian Kolbe
August 14

St. Maximilian Kolbe was a Polish Franciscan priest especially devoted to Our Lady. He gave his life as a martyr of charity in the Auschwitz concentration camp in 1941 when he volunteered to die in place of another prisoner.

Mbaga

June 3

St. Mbaga Tuzinde is one of the most admirable figures among the Uganda martyrs of 1886. An adopted son of the chief executioner, he was freed from his chains and sent back home. In spite of the entreaties of his family, he broke away from their loving caresses and returned to force his father to execute him with his companions. When his father failed to convince him to leave his faith, he ordered the young man's neck to be broken with a club before his body was put on the stake to be burned.

MEINRAD

(Teutonic: Strong Firmness)
January 21
Another Form: Maynard

St. Meinrad was born into a noble family in what is now Germany about 800. He became a monk and a priest at the Abbey of Reichenau, where he taught Sacred Scripture. Feeling that monastic life was not strict enough for him, he received permission to live as a hermit. For seven years he lived on a mountain peak overlooking Lake Zurich. He left to make a hermitage in a remote forest, taking with him a statue of the Virgin. The spot is now a place of pilgrimage to Our Lady of Einsiedeln, Meinrad's statue. St. Meinrad was killed in 861 by bandits.

MEL

(Gaelic, from Latin: Honey)
February 6
Another Form: Melvin

St. Mel is one of the earliest Irish saints. He was a nephew of St. Patrick, whom he assisted in his work. He became a priest and was appointed the first bishop of Armagh. He built a great monastery at Armagh, and he served as abbot. He was the one who received the great St. Brigit into the religious life. He died about 490.

MICHAEL

(Hebrew: Who Is Like God?)
September 29
Other Forms: Michel, Michele, Miguel, Mike, Mikhail, Mitchell

St. Michael the Archangel is one of the three angels mentioned by name in the Bible. The Prophet Daniel describes him as the heavenly prince who stands guard over God's people. He is considered the leader of God's powers against Satan. Michael has always been popular with Christians of both East and West. Many churches have been built in his honor, and one of the most famous, Mont Saint Michel, was erected in Normandy, France, in 709. He is patron of policemen and of the armed services.

ST. MICHAEL THE ARCHANGEL

BLESSED MIGUEL PRO, S.J.
November 23

Blessed Miguel was born in 1891 in Guadalupe, Zacatecas, Mexico. The son of a mining director, Miguel as a child was full of happiness. He entered the Jesuit novitiate in 1911. Because of the turbulent political situation of the country, the Jesuits were expelled and Miguel continued his studies in the United States, Nicaragua, Spain, and Belgium, where he was finally ordained. In 1926 he returned to Mexico where he carried out a hidden apostolate as the churches were closed and the Catholics were suffering severe persecution. He was arrested on a trumped-up charge and without benefit of any legal due process was executed by a firing squad in November of 1927. His last words were clearly heard: "Viva Cristo Rey!" (Long Live Christ the King). He was beatified in 1988 as the first of this century's wave of martyrs from Mexico to be so honored.

MOSES

(Hebrew: Saved From Water)
August 28
Other Forms: Moise, Mose

St. Moses is one of the earliest recorded black saints. Born in Abyssinia as a slave, he had a vile temper and nasty disposition. He became so troublesome and mean that as a young man he was driven from his master's estate. He then became a robber and headed up a band of highwaymen that preyed upon travelers going to and from Egypt. Somehow (the details are lost) he was converted to Christianity, and his life then became one of penance. He joined a monastery in Lower Egypt, became a priest, and was one of the foremost Fathers of the Desert. He had many disciples when he died near the end of the fifth century.

Mugagga

June 3

St. Mugagga was a teenager among the Uganda martyrs. A page in the service of the debauched king of Buganda, he is a heroic example of youthful chastity. Mugagga was burned to death June 3, 1886.

Mukasa

June 3

St. Mukasa Kiriwawanvu was a Christian catechumen who had been sent to jail for a dispute with St. Gyavira. At the time of departure for Namugongo, the place where a group of the Uganda martyrs were to be burned, Mukasa was taken to the cell where the others were waiting. Immediately, Gyavira welcomed him as a friend, forgiving his past injury. Witnesses testified that until the end only the sound of praying was heard; not a single lament was made. St. Mukasa was burned to death in 1886.

Nathaniel

(Hebrew: Gift of God)
August 24
Other Forms: Nate, Nathanael, Nathan

Nathaniel is believed to be another name for St. Bartholomew the Apostle. It was not uncommon for a Jew to have two names and to be known by either or both of them. He is introduced under this name when the Apostle Philip brings him to Jesus, who confounds him with what He already knows. Jesus promises Nathaniel that he will see great things. This account is recorded in the first chapter of the Gospel of John.

NICHOLAS

(Greek: People's Victory)
December 6
Other Forms: Claus, Cohn, Klaus, Nick, Nicol, Nicola, Nikolaus, Niles, Nils

St. Nicholas is one of the most popular saints of the early Church, and many early writers speak of his greatness. There are many stories of miracles he worked in his lifetime. After some years as a monk, he became archbishop of Myra, Turkey. One story told about him relates to the time he was on his way to the Council of Nicaea. He stopped at an inn to spend the night where the owner had killed two boys to steal from them the little money they carried. Nicholas discovered the crime, brought the boys back to life, and had the innkeeper arrested. For this and other acts he is considered the patron of children. He is the one who supposedly brought presents to children at Christmas, whom children today call Santa Claus (Saint Claus, or Nicholas). He died about 324.

Other saints with this name:

ST. NICHOLAS OF TOLENTINE (ITALY)
September 10

ST. NICHOLAS OF UMBRIA (ITALY)
October 10

NOAH

(Hebrew: Peace)
Another Form: Noe

In the Old Testament, Noah is the son of Lamech, descended from Adam. According to the Bible, God became angry with the people of the world for their corrupt ways, and he decided to send a great flood to cover the world and destroy mankind. But Noah found favor in God's eyes, and God instructed Noah to build a great ark, a huge boat, and to take his wife and his sons and their wives onto the boat along with two of every animal on earth. The people around Noah laughed at him, but when the rains came, Noah and his family and the animals boarded the ark and were spared. The flood lasted forty days and forty nights. The story of Noah and the flood begins in Genesis, chapter six.

St. Noe Mawaggali
June 3

St. Noe Mawaggali was one of the Ugandan martyrs. A potter, he was executed during the persecution of King Mwanga. He was known for his Christian poverty.

Noel

(French: Christmas)
February 21

Blessed Noel Pinot was a martyr in the French revolution. One of sixteen children, he became a priest in 1771. For a time he served as a chaplain of a hospital and then became a pastor, using the income from his parish to aid the poor. When the revolutionary tribunal told him to take the oath to the revolutionary government, which was opposed to the Church, Noel refused. Driven from his parish, he was forced to go into hiding. He did not desert his people but hid by day and said Mass and heard confession by night. One night as he was saying Mass at a farm, he was discovered and arrested. He was sentenced to death and on February 21, 1794, he had his head chopped off by the guillotine.

Norbert

(French: Brightness)
June 6

St. Norbert was a handsome young man of noble German birth who allowed himself to become a subdeacon in order to gain ecclesiastical honors. He led a worldly life until he was thirty-three years old. While riding one day he was struck by lightning and, because of this close brush with death, he gave away his possessions, became a priest, dressed in poor clothes, and went about preaching against the life he had once led. Accused by enemies of slandering the clergy, Norbert was brought before Pope Gelasius, who heard his story and authorized him to preach anywhere in the Catholic Church. With some friends he founded the Premonstratensian Order to restore religious life among clergy and people. He was later made a bishop, and he died in 1134.

OLIVER

(Latin: Peace)
July 10
Other Forms: Olivier, Ollie

St. Oliver Plunkett was born in Ireland during the time James I and Oliver Cromwell of England were trying to make the country Protestant. Because of the lack of educational opportunities for Irish boys, he was sent to the Irish College in Rome when he was sixteen. There he became a priest and worked in the Holy City until Pope Clement IX named him archbishop of Armagh. In Ireland he worked under great difficulty because of persecution by the English. Finally he was accused by renegades of conspiracy against the British. He was taken to England and put on trial. The witnesses against him perjured themselves and told fantastic lies. It was enough for the British to condemn him to death. He greeted his sentence of hanging by saying, "It is good for me at this time to give an example to the Irish people since I have already given them so much advice." He was executed at the infamous Tyburn Prison in 1681.

OTTO

(Teutonic: Rich)
July 2
Other Forms: Odo, Odilo, Otho

St. Otto was a priest who became chancellor of the German Empire. He was a friend of kings and popes. When King Boleslaus conquered Pomerania, he called for missioners to preach the Gospel there.

Otto and some companions answered the call and went to Pomerania (Poland). In one year Otto baptized twenty thousand people and built eleven churches. He died in 1139.

OWEN

(Middle English: To Possess)
March 3

St. Owen was an Anglo-Saxon monk who with St. Chad worked to serve the people of England, particularly the poor. He labored in the area of Lichfield. St. Owen led a very holy life and is reputed to have had visions of Jesus and heaven. He died about 680, and the people among whom he worked proclaimed him a saint.

PASCAL

(Hebrew: Passover)
May 17
Other Forms: Paschal, Pasquale

St. Pascal Baylon was born in Aragon (Spain) in 1540.From the time he was a boy until he became a young man, he was a shepherd. When he was about twenty-seven he became a Franciscan Brother, serving as cook, gardener, and porter. He served the poor in many ways but particularly by his healing powers. He worked many miracles, and during the process of canonization St. Robert Bellarmine told the court, "His like has not been seen in the world." Because of his devotion to the Holy Eucharist, Pope Leo XIII named him special patron of Eucharistic congresses.

PATRICK

(Latin: Nobly Born)
March 17
Other Forms: Padraic, Pat, Patrice, Patricio

St. Patrick was born in Great Britain about 885. When he was about sixteen, he was captured by pirates and taken to Ireland as a slave,

ST. PATRICK

working as a shepherd. Patrick escaped and returned home. The paganism of Ireland disturbed Patrick, and he resolved to become a priest and to return there to preach the Gospel. When he did go back, it was as a bishop. Patrick went to Tara, which was the seat of the Irish kings and the pagan Druid priests. It was at the time of the vernal equinox when all the fires in Ireland were supposed to be extinguished until the Druids made new fire. On a hill overlooking Tara, Patrick built a huge bonfire to announce the Resurrection. The next day he went to Tara and debated the Druids, whom he overcame. Then plucking a shamrock from the ground, he used its three leaves to explain the Trinity to the kings. Patrick was tireless in preaching the Gospel, and he converted many, many thousands to the Faith. St. Patrick organized the Church through Ireland, lived a life of penance, and wrote many prayers (some of which still remain for us). He died in 461.

PAUL

(Latin: Little)
June 29
Other Forms: Pablo, Paolo, Paulinus, Paulo, Pawel

Paul was born in Tarsus, Cilicia, a fact which gave him Roman citizenship. His parents, devout Jews, sent him to Jerusalem to study his religion under the noted Rabbi Gamaliel. There he became a Pharisee. Because of his deep Jewish religious beliefs, he opposed Christianity. He was present approvingly at the stoning to death of Stephen the Deacon, the first martyr. He was on his way to Damascus to arrest Christians when he was struck to the ground and Christ appeared to him. From that moment on he devoted himself entirely to the spread of Christianity. Along with Peter he became the leading figure in the early Church, and no one did as much as he to shape Christianity. His missionary journeys took him through Asia Minor, Greece, the Mediterranean islands, and finally to Rome as a prisoner. Attempts were made on his life; he was imprisoned and beaten. He was freed from his first Roman imprisonment. Then he was rearrested by agents of Nero and taken again to Rome, where because he was a Roman citizen he was beheaded, not crucified, about three years after St. Peter. His many epistles give the basis for Catholic teaching. According to Eusebius, he was martyred in the year 67.

Other saints with this name:

ST. PAUL MIKI (JAPAN)
February 6

St. Paul of Damascus (Syria)
September 25

St. Paulinus of Nola (Italy)
June 22

St. Paul of Rome (Italy)
June 26

Peter

(Greek: Rock)
June 29
Other Forms: Pedro, Perrin, Pete, Petrus, Pier, Pierce, Pierre, Piers, Pietro, Piotr

It was at the Jordan River that Simon bar Jonah first met Jesus. He was there with his brother Andrew, who first told him about Jesus. Simon and Andrew were fishermen from Bethsaida, a town on the north shore of the Sea of Galilee. When Jesus began His public life, He called Simon and Andrew to follow Him. Jesus changed the former's name from Simon to Peter, telling him that he was the rock on which He would found His Church. Peter was present at all the important Gospel incidents and was chosen by Jesus to witness His Transfiguration. Peter began Christ's Passion boldly enough, cutting off the ear of one who would arrest Jesus. Then he became afraid and three times denied that he even knew Christ. Jesus forgave him and after the Resurrection three times ordered Peter to take care of the people in the Church. On Pentecost, Peter was the chief spokesman for the Apostles. The Acts of the Apostles tell of his miracles and leadership. He was arrested about 43 by Herod but miraculously released. He presided over the Council of Jerusalem in the year 50, when it was decided to admit Gentiles to the Church. He became the first bishop of Antioch, lived for a time in Corinth, then went to Rome, where he was crucified upside down during the persecution of Nero. His tomb is beneath the main altar of St. Peter's Basilica in Rome. He was the first pope, and the Church holds that his successors have the same powers as Christ gave Peter, which are necessary to guide the Church with which Christ promised to remain until the end of time.

BLESSED PETER TO ROT
July 7

Blessed Peter To Rot was a young married man and father and a lay catechist in New Guinea during World War II. When the Japanese military forces arrived to occupy his island, they interred the missionary priests and harassed Peter, jailing him more than once. They legalized polygamy and made rules to limit the Catholic presence among the native people. Peter openly opposed the regulations and the practice of polygamy, defending the faith he would not deny. He was jailed again and singled out for harsh treatment. He asked his wife to bring his best clothes to jail so that he could go to God properly dressed. About a month before the Japanese surrendered, Peter was murdered by a lethal injection, held down while he died in agony. Although the Japanese tried to pass off the murder as a natural death, there was a witness who later testified to Peter's heroic defense of the faith. Pope John Paul II beatified this admirable catechist in 1995.

BLESSED PIER GIORGIO FRASSATI
July 4

A young Italian mining student of our own century, Blessed Pier contracted polio in 1925 while visiting an abandoned sick person, and he faced the terminal illness with calm, patience, and holy resolve. Just before his death, he wrote, "We should always be cheerful. Sadness should be banished from all Christian souls." When Pope John Paul II beatified Pier in 1990, he spoke of him as a "joyful, enthusiastic apostle of Christ, a passionate follower of his message and charity."

Other saints with this name

ST. PETER BAPTIST (JAPAN)
February 6

ST. PETER CANISIUS (SWITZERLAND)
April 27

ST. PETER CHANEL (OCEANIA)
April 28

ST. PETER DAMIAN (ITALY)
February 21

ST. PETER NOLASCO (SPAIN)
January 31

ST. PETER

PHILIP

(Greek: Lover of Horses)
Other Forms: Felipe, Filippo, Phelps, Philipp, Philippe, Philippus

ST. PHILIP THE APOSTLE
May 3

St. Philip, a native of Bethsaida, was in Galilee when Jesus called upon him to become His follower. It was Philip who told Nathaniel that he had found the one of whom Moses had written. Nathaniel replied, "Can anything good come from Nazareth?" Philip brought Nathaniel to Jesus, who won him over and made him the Apostle Bartholomew. Philip was the one who helped Jesus at the miracle of feeding the five thousand. Jesus tested Philip by asking him how they were to feed the large crowd. Philip told Jesus that there was a boy in the crowd with a few loaves and fishes, adding, "What is that among so many?" Jesus sent Philip for the boy and with these few loaves and fishes fed the large crowd. At the Last Supper, Philip asked Jesus to show the Apostles the Father. Jesus told Philip, "He who sees me, sees the Father." We do not know how or when St. Philip died.

ST. PHILIP NERI
May 26

St. Philip Neri, sometimes called the Apostle of Rome, was born in Florence. He was a gifted man who was skilled in law, chemistry, poetry, music, psychology, and theology. He went to Rome in 1536, laboring there as a lay missioner, working with youth, preaching, visiting hospitals, converting rich and poor, a favorite of intellectuals. He helped found the noted Oratory and the Oratorians. He became a priest in 1551. He was so happy in life that he used to cry out, "Enough, Lord! Enough!" He died in 1595.

PIUS

(Latin: Holy)
August 21
Another Form: Pio

Pius is the name of a number of popes of whom three are saints, the latest being Pope St. Pius X. He was born near Venice in 1835, became a priest, bishop of Mantua, and then patriarch of Venice. He was elected pope in 1908. He opposed the errors of Modernism that were sweeping the Church at the time, promoted Gregorian Chant, encouraged frequent Holy Communion, and insisted that children be given the sacrament at the age of reason. His whole pontificate was aimed at restoring all things in Christ. He died in 1914.

QUENTIN

(Latin: Fifth)
October 31
Other Forms: Quin, Quincy, Quinn, Quintus

St. Quentin was the son of a Roman senator. He went with St. Lucian to France to preach the Gospel. He was arrested and imprisoned in Amiens. When he refused to deny Christ, he was tortured and beheaded in a place that afterwards was given his name. He died about 285. In 641, St. Eligius discovered his body and built a handsome tomb for it. St. Quentin is invoked against coughs.

RALPH

(Teutonic: Good Omen)
July 7
Other Forms: Rafe, Rafello, Ratoul, Raul, Rolte, Rodolfo, Rudolf, Rudolph, Rodolphus

Blessed Ralph Milner was a poor farmer who could not read or write, the father of eight children. He was converted from Protestantism and was arrested on the day of his First Communion. The English judge said that he would free Ralph because of his age and his large number of children if he would go to a nearby Anglican church and say his prayers. Ralph refused, as this would seem that he was denying his new faith. He was executed for his religion at Winchester, England, on July 7, 1591.

RAPHAEL

(Hebrew: God's Healer)
September 29
Other Forms: Rafael, Rafaelle, Raffaello

St. Raphael is one of the three archangels mentioned in the Bible. His story is found in the Book of Tobit. When Tobit decided to send his son, Tobias, or Tobiah, to Media to collect a debt, he hired a young man, Azariah, to go along as guide. The journey was made successfully with many adventures, during which the debt was collected. Tobias found a bride and a fortune, and his father had his sight restored. The mysterious young man was the cause of all this good luck. When Tobit wanted to pay him handsomely, the young man declined a reward and revealed: "I am Raphael, one of the seven holy angels who present the prayers of the saints and who enters into the presence of the glory of the holy one." He said that he had come because God had sent him and that he was returning to God. After that, Tobit and Tobias saw him no more.

RAYMOND

(Teutonic: Wise Protection)
Other Forms: Raimondo, Ramon, Ray, Raymund, Redmond

ST. RAYMOND OF PENYAFORT
January 7

St. Raymond was a Spaniard who joined the Dominican Order, of which he eventually became head. He was a very learned man in law and wrote a number of works. After a holy and devout life, he died in 1275.

St. Raymond Nonnatus
August 31

St. Raymond was horn in Spain and given the baptismal name of Raymond, to which was added Nonnatus (not born) because he came into the world through a Caesarian operation and not in the usual manner. He joined the Mercedarian Order, which St. Peter Nolasco had recently founded to rescue captives from the Muslims. He raised ransom money by begging and personally redeemed hundreds of captives in Valencia, Algiers, and Tunisia. In the last place, he ran out of money and gave himself up as a captive in order to free a Christian. After eight months of cruel slave treatment, he himself was rescued by other members of his order. After his release, he urged St. Louis of France to lead a crusade. He was later made a cardinal, and he died in 1240. St. Raymond is patron of infants, midwives, and mothers about to give birth.

Reginald

(Teutonic: Strong Judgment)
February 17
Other Forms: Reggie, Reinhold, Reinwald, Reynold, Rinaldo, Ronald

Blessed Reginald of Orléans was the first member of the Dominican Order to die. He was born near Aries, France, in 1183. He taught canon law at the University of Paris. While making a pilgrimage to Rome, he met St. Dominic and became his follower. He founded the Dominican priory in Bologna. He was a great preacher and made many recruits for the new Dominican Order. He died in Paris on February, 1270.

Rene

(French: Reborn)
October 19
Other Forms: Renato, Renatus

St. Rene Goupil was a Jesuit Oblate who accompanied St. Isaac Jogues when he entered New York State to preach the Gospel. Captured by Mohawk Indians, he and St. Isaac were taken to Auriesville and subjected to cruel torture. He was kept as a slave, but his owner, angered by his prayers, tomahawked him to death in 1642.

RICHARD

(Old English: Firm Ruler)
April 3
Other Forms: Reichart, Ricardo, Riccardo, Rick, Ricky

St. Richard of Chichester was born into a noble but poor family near Worcester, England. After restoring the family fortune and giving his own share to his brother, he went to Europe to study law. Upon his return to England, he was made chancellor of Oxford University and legal advisor to St. Edmund, archbishop of Canterbury. Later he studied theology and became a priest. He was elected bishop of Chichester, selling his goods to help the poor and sick. St. Richard was preaching a crusade to recover the burial place of Christ when he fell ill and died in 1253.

Another saint with this name:

ST. RICHARD GWYNN (ENGLAND)
October 25

ROBERT

(Teutonic: Bright Flame)
September 17
Other Forms: Bob, Roberto, Robin, Rupert, Ruprecht

St. Robert Bellarmine was a bishop and is honored as Doctor (Teacher) of the Church. He was born in 1542 in Tuscany, Italy. A brilliant student, he entered the Society of Jesus and became a priest. He taught for many years at the Roman College and was recognized as one of the great theologians of the Church and a defender against Protestant teachings, He was made a cardinal and was a papal advisor. He died in 1621.

Roderic

(Teutonic: Noble Ruler)
March 13
Other Forms: Rod, Roderick, Roderico, Rodrigo, Rurik

St. Roderic was a priest of Cabra, Spain. It was during the time when the Muslims controlled much of the country. He was betrayed by his brother who had become a Muslim and accused him falsely of deserting the Islamic faith. Roderic told his judge that he was a Christian and had always been a Christian. The judge threw him into prison, telling him that he must deny Christianity. When Roderic continued to refuse to deny his religion, the judge ordered his head to be cut off. He died in 857.

Roger

(Teutonic: Famous Spear)
July 7
Other Forms: Hodge, Rogelio, Rory, Rudiger, Ruggiero

Blessed Roger Dickenson was a native of Lincoln, England, who in order to become a priest had to go to the English College in Rheims, France, because all English seminaries had been closed by the persecution. He had himself smuggled back into England and served the Catholics in the Winchester area. He was caught once but escaped when his guards began drinking. The second time he was arrested along with Blessed Ralph Milner, a lay helper. Both men were executed at Winchester on July 7, 1591.

Romanus

(Latin: Roman)
February 28
Other Forms: Romain, Roman, Romano, Romaric, Romeo

St. Romanus was born in what is now France. He was thirty-five when he entered a monastery in Lyons. Not finding the life severe enough, he left to become a hermit in a remote area. Later he was joined by his brother and then a sister, and three monasteries were founded by them. He is said to have worked many miracles. One day he met two lepers on the road and embraced them. After he had gone on, the lepers were surprised to see that they had been healed and were no longer disfigured. He died about 463. He is prayed to for people with mental illness.

RONALD

(Scottish form of Reginald, Teutonic: Strong Judgment)
August 20
Other Forms: Ron, Ronaldo, Ronnie, Aldo

St. Ronald was a British chieftain of Orkney. He built the Cathedral of St. Magnusin Kirkwall. He was killed by rebels in 1158. Because of the holiness of his life, many miracles are said to have taken place in his name following his death.

RUDOLPH

(Teutonic: Famous Wolf)
Other Forms: Rolfe, Rodolfo, Rodolphus, Rudolf, Rudy

Blessed Rudolf was the son of the duke of Atri, Spain, who joined the Jesuit Society at the age of eighteen. After his ordination, he was sent to preach the Gospel in the region of Agra, India. Later he was transferred to an area north of Bombay. Here the Hindus gave great opposition. Blessed Rudolf decided to build a church in the village of Cuncolim, where the opposition was the strongest. Together with some other Jesuits and Indian laymen, he went there on July 15, 1583. Hindus ambushed them, killing the members of the party with arrows.

RUPERT

(Teutonic: Bright Flame)
March 27
Other Forms: Robert, Ruprecht

St. Rupert was a French priest who was appointed bishop of Worms, Germany. Some people in power resented him and drove him from his see. He then preached Christianity in Bavaria and Upper Germany, making many converts. With this success he established his see at what is now Salzburg, Austria. There he died on Easter Sunday, 718.

SALVATORE

(Latin: Savior)
Other Forms: Sal, Salvador, Salvator

This name is from the title given to Our Lord Jesus Christ, Savior, and most people who receive this name have been given it in honor of Jesus. It can be celebrated on any feast of Our Lord but is most appropriate at Easter.

SALVATOR OF HORTA
March 18

St. Salvator of Horta is one of the great wonder-workers of the Church. He began life as a shepherd, then became a shoemaker and finally a Franciscan Brother. As a Brother he served as a cook and porter. He is reputed to have had great healing powers, working many miracles. People came from all over Spain to seek his aid. He died in 1567. He is a patron of shoemakers.

SAMUEL

(Hebrew: Asked of the Lord)
August 20
Another Form: Sam, Samuele

Samuel was one of the great prophets of the Old Testament, and his story is recorded in the First Book of Kings. His mother, Anna, had long been childless, and she promised God that if He gave her a son she would dedicate him to His work. God heard her prayer, and Samuel was born. Anna took Samuel, while still a boy, to the high priest, Eli, to serve him and be educated. It was while serving Eli that Samuel was called by God to be His prophet. Samuel became a Judge of Israel, selected Saul to be King, and when Saul failed, replaced him with the great King David.

St. Sebastian

SEBASTIAN

(Greek: Venerable)
January 20

Sebastian was born in Milan and went to Rome to enlist in the army, where he hoped he could help fellow Christians who were being persecuted. He first saved the brothers Marcus and Marcellinus, who had been condemned to death, by speaking so fervently of Christ that he converted the jailer, the clerk of the prefecture, the parents of the condemned men, and sixteen prisoners. These conversions led to the conversion of the governor of Rome, who released the prisoners. During this time Sebastian was such a good soldier that Emperor Diocletian made him a captain of the Praetorian Guard. He was finally discovered and delivered up to the archers. When arrows failed to kill him, he was beaten to death and his body thrown into a sewer. He died about 288.

SIGMUND

(Teutonic: Victorious Protector)
May 1
Other Forms: Siegmund, Sigismondo, Sigismund

Sigmund is a diminutive form of Sigismund, a king of Burgundy (France). He ruled for only one year, during which time he allowed his son to be put to death. Filled with remorse, he resigned as king and founded a monastery, to which he retired to live a life of penance. He was seized by an enemy chieftain and put to death in 524. He is honored as a martyr, and a shrine was built to his memory in Bohemia (Prague).

SIMON

(Hebrew: Obedient)
October 28
Other Forms: Simeon, Simone

St. Simon was an Apostle who was also known as The Zealot to distinguish him from St. Simon Peter, who had the same first name until Jesus changed it. He was a native of Cana and may have been a member of the political-religious group called Zealots, or perhaps he got the name from his personal zeal. Tradition says he preached the Gospel in Persia and was martyred there.

Other saints with this name:

ST. SIMON OF CYRENE (PALESTINE)
December 1

ST. SIMON STOCK (ENGLAND)
May 16

STANISLAUS

(Slavic: Military Glory)
April 11
Other Forms: Stan, Stanislao, Stanislas, Stanley

St. Stanislaus is honored as a bishop and martyr. He was born in Poland and educated at the University of Paris. He became bishop at a time Poland was ruled by King Boleslaus, a mighty warrior whose personal life was very sinful. Stanislaus threatened to excommunicate the king unless he remedied his evil ways. For a time the king seemed to reform, but after defeating the Russians at Kiev, Boleslaus returned home victorious and popular, thinking he was bigger than the Church. Once again he returned to his evil life. Stanislaus gave him several warnings and then for the good of souls excommunicated him. The king refused to accept the excommunication and turned up for Mass. St. Stanislaus refused to celebrate Mass in the cathedral but went to a small church outside the city. Boleslaus followed him there and ordered his soldiers to arrest the bishop. When they held back because of respect, Boleslaus took his sword and split the saint's head open. The year was 1079.

Another saint with this name:

ST. STANISLAUS KOSTKA (POLAND)
August 15

STEPHEN

(Greek: Crowned)

Other Forms: Esteban, Stefan, Stefano, Stefen, Stephan, Steve, Steven, Sven

ST. STEPHEN THE MARTYR
December 26

St. Stephen is the first martyr of the Church, patron of smelters and stonecutters. He was a disciple in the early Church who was selected to become a deacon. The Acts of the Apostles describe him as a man "full of grace and power, who did great wonders and signs among the people." He debated with the Jews in their synagogues, and when they could not stand up against his wisdom, they accused him falsely to the chief priests. He was arrested and taken before the Jewish council. The Acts of the Apostles records his sermon before the council. The Jews, however, stopped up their ears, dragged him outside the walls, and stoned him. As they were stoning him, Stephen prayed: "Lord Jesus, receive my spirit" and "Lord, do not hold this sin against them." So praying, he died. Among those at the stoning was a man named Saul, who later was converted and become St. Paul.

ST. STEPHEN OF HUNGARY
August 16

When St. Stephen became a Christian, he took for his baptismal name that of the first martyr. He was crowned king of Hungary in the year 1000 when he was twenty years old. He was a just king who strove to convert his subjects to the Church, earning from the pope the title of Apostolic King. He dedicated his country to the Blessed Virgin. St. Stephen died in 1038, and his crown is the most precious relic in Hungary today.

TERENCE

(Latin: Smooth)
April 10
Other Forms: Terrence, Terry

St. Terence was a martyr who died in Carthage during the persecution of Decius, about 250. Nothing else is known of him.

THADDEUS

(Aramaic: Wise)
October 28

Thaddeus is another name for St. Jude the Apostle, who is known as Jude Thaddeus.

THEODORE

(Greek: God's Gift)
February 7
Other Forms: Feodor, Tad, Ted, Teddy, Teodoro, Theo, Theodotius

Theodore was a member of a Roman legion stationed in the East. He was denounced as a Christian. Theodore was given his release with a warning. Despite this, he set fire to a pagan temple and was again arrested. This time Theodore was ordered to deny his Christian faith. When he refused, he was tortured by having his flesh torn. Still refusing to recant, he was put to death by being burned about the year 319.

THOMAS

(Aramaic: Twin)
July 3
Other Forms: Didymus, Tomas, Tommaso

When Jesus was preparing to return to the vicinity of Jerusalem the last time before His death, it was Thomas who exclaimed to the

St. Thomas

other Apostles, "Let us also go and die with Him." Thomas, also called Didymus (the twin), was not with the other Apostles when Jesus appeared to them after the Resurrection. When they told him about their experience, Thomas refused to believe, saying, "Unless I place my finger in the mark of the nails, and my hand in His side, I will not believe." Eight days later Jesus appeared again and called Thomas to put his finger in the nail holes and his hand in His side, adding: "Do not be faithless but believing." Thomas answered: "My Lord and my God."

According to tradition Thomas preached the Gospel as far away as India, where he was martyred. He is the patron of architects and masons.

St. Thomas Aquinas
January 28

St. Thomas Aquinas is a Doctor (Teacher) of the Church and patron of Catholic schools. He became a Dominican friar, studied under St. Albert the Great, and taught in universities in Cologne, Bologna, and Paris. He has been called the Church's most outstanding writer and teacher of philosophy and theology, and he left behind a large library of writings. He died on the way to the Council of Lyons in 1369.

St. Thomas Becket
December 29

Born in London, Thomas was selected by Henry II to be his chancellor of England. He lived in luxury and power, a close friend and confidant of the king. When the episcopal see of Canterbury became vacant, Henry named his friend to be the archbishop. Thomas was ordained a priest and consecrated a bishop. He immediately changed his life from luxury to austerity. He felt that there was a conflict of interest between his roles as leading churchman and chancellor, so he resigned the latter post, to the anger of Henry. He further angered Henry by siding with the pope in a dispute with the king. Henry sent him into exile. When he was permitted to return, Henry counted on his friendship and obedience. But again Thomas protected the interests of the Church and the pope. "Won't someone rid me of this insolent priest?" Henry exclaimed in anger. Some henchmen heard him and went to the cathedral, where they found Thomas at prayer and there in 1170 murdered him.

St. Thomas More
June 22

St. Thomas More was the chancellor of England under King Henry VIII. When the king broke with the pope because he would not grant him a divorce, Thomas refused to join the new Church of England. He was tried for treason and found guilty. Condemned to death by behead-

St. Thomas Becket

ing, Thomas joked with his executioners, even removing his beard from the execution block, saying that it had not committed treason and didn't deserve to be cut. St. Thomas was an educated and humorous man who had a deep spirituality and loyalty to the papacy. He died in 1535.

TIMOTHY

(Greek: God-Fearing)
January 26
Other Forms: Tim, Timon, Timoteo, Timotheus

Timothy was a convert of St. Paul who later became his close friend and companion. Two letters that St. Paul wrote to his beloved Timothy can be found in the New Testament. Timothy traveled with Paul through the Near East, to Greece and Rome. He also took missionary journeys alone. St. Paul charged him: "Preach the word, be urgent in season and out of season, convince, rebuke, and exhort." In his last letter to Timothy, Paul writes that he is at the point of being sacrificed, saying, "I have fought the good fight, I have finished the race, I have kept the faith." He urges Timothy to hurry to him before winter comes. Later Timothy became a bishop of the Church at Ephesus, and tradition says that he was stoned to death during a pagan feast.

TITUS

(Latin: Safe)
January 4
Another Form: Tito

St. Titus was a gentile convert who assisted St. Paul the Apostle. St. Paul sent him to both Corinth and Crete to settle problems in the churches there. St. Paul wrote a letter to Titus which is contained in the New Testament (Epistle to Titus). He is honored as the first bishop of the Island of Crete. He died there about the end of the first century.

TOBIAS

(Hebrew: Goodness of God)
November 2
Other Forms: Tobia, Tobiah, Tobit, Toby

St. Tobias was a Christian soldier in the army of the Emperor Licinius and was stationed in Armenia. When the soldiers were ordered to take part in a sacrifice to pagan gods, Tobias and some other Christians refused. They were burned at the stake for their refusal about the year 315. (There is also a Biblical figure named Tobias, and his story is in the Book of Tobit.)

URBAN

(Latin: Man of the City)
May 25
Other Forms: Urbano, Urbanus

Urban is the name for a number of popes, bishops, and martyrs. The first pope who is a saint with this name is Pope St. Urban I, who is honored as a martyr. He succeeded St. Callistus as pope in 223 and ruled the Church during a period of persecution, working to help those who were arrested. Among the martyrs he helped was St. Cecilia. He died in 230.

VALERIUS

(Latin: Valiant)
February 14
Other Forms: Balentin, Valeno, Valens, Valentine, Valentino, Valentinus, Valerian, Valeriano

Valerius, or Valentine, was a priest in Rome. He was arrested and taken before the Emperor Claudius the Goth, to whom he confessed his faith and denounced the pagan gods Jupiter and Mercury. He was turned over to a magistrate named Asterius, who had a blind daughter. Valentine converted Asterius and his family when he restored sight to the blind girl. He was reported again to the emperor for these conversions, and Claudius ordered him decapitated on the Flaminian Way about 270. Pope Nicholas I built a church in his honor, and it became a place of pilgrimage. He is the patron of engaged couples.

VICTOR

(Latin: Winner)
July 21
Other Forms: Vic, Victorio, Vittorio

Victor was an officer in the army stationed in Marseilles. When Maximianus Herculius arrived in the city, the Christians were very worried because that general had just massacred the Theban Legion for being Christian. Victor was exhorting his Christian soldiers to be firm when he was caught in the act. He was taken before the prefects of the legion, who told him to be faithful to the gods and not to a dead man named Jesus. The prefects sent him to Maximianus, who ordered him to be dragged through the streets of the city, tortured on the rack, and finally crushed to death under a millstone. He died about 287. He is the patron of cabinetmakers and is invoked against lightning.

VINCENT

(Latin: Conquering)
Other Forms: Vince, Vincente, Vincenzo, Vincintius

ST. VINCENT THE DEACON
January 22

St. Vincent is a martyr who has had great popularity throughout Europe. He was a deacon who was assistant to the Bishop Valerius in what is now Spain. When the persecutions of Emperor Diocletian began, the Roman governor of the province had Valerius and Vincent arrested. Because the bishop was old, Vincent asked to speak for him. This made the governor angry. He ordered that Vincent's flesh be cut with iron hooks and then that the deacon be roasted over a slow fire. Vincent prayed and sang psalms until he died. He is the patron of wine-growers. He died about 305.

St. Vincent Ferrer
April 5

St. Vincent Ferrer was born in Valencia, Spain, and took his name from the deacon-martyr St. Vincent, who had been put to death there by the Romans. He entered the Dominican order and soon became noted for his preaching and faith healing, working many miracles. His preach-

St. Vincent De Paul

ing took him throughout Spain, France, Switzerland, and Italy. He is reputed to have converted many lukewarm Catholics. He died in 1419. He is the patron of construction workers.

St. Vincent De Paul
September 27

One of the great figures of the French Church, St. Vincent was born into a laboring-class family in the south of France about 1580. As a boy he tended sheep and did farm chores. Because he was intelligent and wished to become a priest, his father resolved to help him and sold two oxen to pay for his education. He became a priest and strove for worldly honors. On a journey along the coast of France, he was captured by Barbary (Muslim) pirates and taken as prisoner to Tunis. He escaped for a return to France and honors, becoming almoner of the queen and holder of many benefices. Then in 1617 he renounced all his honors and became a great saint and Apostle. To the rich and poor, he was simply known as Monsieur Vincent. He labored for the galley slaves and the poor. He founded the Vincentian Order and the Sisters of Charity. His charities became a model for the whole Church. He died in Paris, September 27, 1737.

St. Vincent Liem (Diem) Thi Nguyen
St. Vincent Yen Do

Two of the Vietnamese martyr saints were named Vincent. The priest St. Vincent of Peace Liem was beheaded along with St. Hyacinth Castaneda in 1773. He was the first Dominican martyr of Vietnam. St. Vincent Yen Do, also a priest, was arrested and executed in 1838 after carrying out a hidden ministry. They are honored along with the other Vietnamese martyrs on November 14.

VLADIMIR

(Slovak: World Ruler)
July 15

St. Vladimir was baptized in 987 when he was king of an area that is now part of Russia. He enlarged his kingdom by recovering territory from the Poles, defeating the Bulgars along the Volga River and capturing territories in the north as far as Finland. At the same time he brought Christian missioners from Byzantium (Constantinople) and Germany. He destroyed paganism in the area and brought whole populations into the Church.

WALTER

(Teutonic: Strong Warrior)
April 8
Other Forms: Gualthieri, Walther

St. Walter was born in Picardy, France. He is the patron saint of prisoners because, when he was a novice studying to be a monk, he smuggled bread in to a peasant who was being held a prisoner and at night entered the man's cell to free him from his chains. He was later elected abbot of his monastery, much against his will. Several times he tried to escape his role of abbot, once retiring to the Abbey of Cluny and again making a retreat into the forests. Each time his holiness attracted crowds and he was discovered. Finally, Pope Gregory VII ordered hi4m to fulfill his duties as abbot, which he did for the remainder of his life. He died about 1095.

WENCESLAUS

(Slavic: Great Glory)
September 28
Other Forms: Vinceslao, Wenceslas

Wenceslaus was thirteen when his father, the king of Bohemia, died. His mother, a pagan, ruled until he became eighteen. Wenceslaus

St. Wenceslaus

was trained in Christianity by his grandmother. When he became king, he ended the persecution of the Christians, recalled exiled priests, built churches, and is said to have ground the wheat and made the wine to be used at the Eucharist. Wenceslaus invited his pagan brother, Boleslaus, to join him in celebrating the feast of Sts. Cosmas and Damian. On the way to Mass, Boleslaus had his brother murdered. The people proclaimed Wenceslaus a martyr and he is honored as the patron of Bohemia. He died in 935.

WILFRID

(Old English: Firm Peace)
October 12

St. Wilfrid was a famous bishop of the Anglo-Saxon Church. He became the archbishop of York and was several times exiled from England because he defended the Church against the king. During his banishments he went to Rome and preached the faith in Europe. He is one of the Apostles of Holland and is honored on the Isle of Wight. He died in 709.

WILLIAM

(Teutonic: Strong Helmet)
June 25
Other Forms: Bill, Billy, Guglielmo, Guiliermo, Guillaume, Wilhelm, Will, Willis, Willy

St. William was born in the Piedmont area of Italy. From the time he was a boy he lived a life of penance. He made the famous pilgrimage to the shrine of St. James in Spain barefoot. He founded a number of monasteries for men and women. He died in 1142.

XAVIER

(Arabic: Bright)
December 3
Another Form: Javier

A name given in honor of St. Francis Xavier, patron of the missions.

ZACHARY

(Hebrew: Remembered by God)
November 5
Other Forms: Zaecaria, Zacharias, Zechariah

St. Zachary was the father of St. John the Baptist and the husband of St. Elizabeth. He and his wife lived near Jerusalem. He was a priest who took his turn serving in the Temple. One day while on duty, he had a vision of an angel who told him that he was to have a son whom he should name John. After the vision, he was struck dumb because he doubted the angel, and he did not regain his speech until after John was born and it came time to name the child. When he was able to speak again, he uttered the beautiful Benedictus prayer, which is still part of the liturgy. Zachary's story is in the first chapter of St. Luke's Gospel.

AUTHOR'S NOTE ABOUT THE NAMES IN THIS BOOK:

There are thousands of saints whose names are not in this book. If your name is not included, it may be a nickname, or part of a name, or simply spelled a little differently. If your first name is not included in this list, you may "adopt" a patron saint whose name sounds like yours.

Names in this Book

Aaron, 14
Abram, 15
Adalbert, 18
Adam, 16, 105
Adan, 16
Adeodatus, 29
Adrian, 16-17
Adrien, 16
Afifa, 9
Agostino, 28
Aiphonsus, 21-22
Alain, 17
Alan, 17
Alban, 17
Albano, 34
Alben, 17
Albert,18-19, 128
Alberto, 18
Albin, 17
Albrecht, 18
Alcuin, 19
Aldo, 120
Alec, 19
Alejandro, 19
Alex, 19-20
Alexander, 19-20
Alexei, 20
Alexis, 20
Alfonso, 21
Alistair, 19
Allan, 17
Allen, 17
Alois, 93
Alonzo, 21
Aloys, 21
Aloysius, 21, 93
Alphaeus, 79
Alphonse, 21
Aluigi, 21
Alva, 17
Ambrose, 22, 29, 67, 92
Amos, 23
Andre, 23
Andreas, 23
Andres, 23
Angel, 25
Angelo, 25
Ansel, 25

Anselm, 25
Anselmo, 25
Anthony, 6, 26-28, 72
Antoine, 26
Anton, 26
Antonio, 26, 41
Antony, 26
Armand, 72
Armando, 72
Arnaldo, 28
Arnold, 28
Arnoldo, 28
Asterius, 131
Augustin, 28
Augustine, 22, 28-29
Austin, 28
Barnabas, 29, 94, 96
Barnaby, 29
Barnard, 33
Barney, 29
Barry, 30
Bart, 30
Bartel, 30
Bartholomew, 30, 104, 114
Bartolomeo, 30
Basil, 30, 68
Bede, 31
Ben, 33
Benedetto, 31
Benedict, 30-32, 62, 87
Benjamin, 10, 33
Bennett, 31
Benson, 33
Bernadino, 33
Bernard, 33, 95
Bernardo, 33
Bernhard, 33
Bert, 18, 71
Bill, 137
Billy, 137
Blaise, 34
Blase, 34
Bob, 118
Bonaventure, 34

Boniface, 34-35
Brandon, 36
Brendan, 36
Brenden, 36
Brennan, 36
Brian, 36
Brice, 36-37
Bruce, 36
Bruno, 37, 73
Bryan, 36
Bryant, 19, 36
Bryce, 36
Bryon, 36
Byron, 36
Camille, 37
Camillo, 37
Camillus, 37
Canute, 88
Carl, 39
Carlo, 39
Carlos, 39
Carroll, 39
Casimir, 38
Casper, 38
Cass, 38
Ceferino, 38
Chad, 38-39, 108
Chantal, 64
Charles, 39, 90
Chinue, 10
Chris, 41
Christian, 40
Christophe, 41
Christopher, 40-41
Clair, 42
Clare, 42, 61
Clarence, 42
Clarus, 42
Claude, 42
Claudius, 42
Claus, 105
Clement, 22, 43, 107
Cloud, 42
Clovis, 92-93
Cohn, 105
Cole, 44
Coleman, 44
Colin, 44

Collin, 44
Colman, 43, 89
Colton, 44
Colum, 44
Columba, 43-44, 88
Columban, 43-44
Columbanus, 44
Columbus, 36
Columcille, 44
Concepcion, 9
Connie, 44
Connor, 45
Conor, 45
Constantine, 44, 73
Constantius, 44
Cormac, 45
Corneal, 45
Cornelius, 45
Cosmas, 47, 137
Cristobal, 41
Cristobalito, 41
Cristoforo, 41
Cullen, 44
Cuthbert, 71
Cyr, 46-47
Cyriac, 46
Cyril, 46
Da, 64
Damian, 47, 113, 137
Damiano, 47
Damien, 47-48
Damon, 47
Dan, 49
Dane, 49
Daniel, 49, 65, 101
Darius, 49
David, 49-51
Dean, 51
Denis, 51-52, 94
Dennis, 51
Dethert, 18
Devin, 52
Devinicus, 52
Didymus, 126, 127
Diego, 78, 84-85
Dino, 51
Dion, 51

139

About the Authors

Maryknoll Father Albert Nevins was the former publisher of Our Sunday Visitor. He wrote many books during his tenure at Our Sunday Visitor, nine of which are still in print. They are:

AMERICAN MARTYRS
ANSWERING A FUNDAMENTALIST
CALLED TO SERVE
CATHOLICISM
FATHER SMITH INSTRUCTS JACKSON (REVISION)
LIFE AFTER DEATH
THE LIFE OF JESUS CHRIST
SCRIPTURES OF FAITH
STRANGERS AT YOUR DOOR

Ann Ball is a noted hagiographer with a specialty in modern saints. Some of her other books for Our Sunday Visitor include the popular **Catholic Traditions in Cooking**, **Catholic Traditions in Crafts**, and **Catholic Traditions in the Garden**, as well as **Faces of Holiness**, **A Litany of Saints**, and books on Mary.

OTHER BOOKS ABOUT SAINTS

Faces of Holiness by Ann Ball. The faces and stories of 175 twentieth-century saints and martyrs come to vivid life. 0-87973-**950**-9, paper, $14.95, 272 pp. 0-87973-**919**-7, Poster, 18" x 24", $3.95.

Our SundayVisitor's Encyclopedia of Saints, by Margaret Bunson, Matthew Bunson, and Stephen Bunson. Virtually every person ever declared a saint by the Catholic Church is in this "must have" reference. 0-87973-**588**-0, hardcover, $39.95, 800 pp. 0-87973-**291**-1, CD-ROM, $49.95.

Lives of the Saints You Should Know, by Matthew and Margaret Bunson. Captivating stories of more than a dozen famous and not-so-famous holy men and women. 0-87973-**576**-7, paper, $8.85, 150 pp. Also available, **Lives of the Saints You Should Know Volume 2.** More "heroes with halos" to inspire and challenge youth and adults. 0-87973-**753**-0, paper, $8.95, 160 pp.

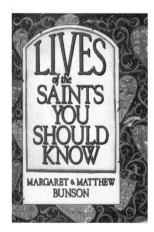

FROM OUR SUNDAY VISITOR 1-800-348-2440
OR HTTP://WWW.OSV.COM